D0323650

MANAGING

COASTAL

EROSION

Committee on Coastal Erosion Zone Management
Water Science and Technology Board
Marine Board
Commission on Engineering and Technical Systems
National Research Council

NATIONAL ACADEMY PRESS
Washington, D.C. 1990

National Academy Press • 2101 Constitution Avenue, N.W. • Washington, D.C. 20418

NOTICE: The project that is the subject of this report was approved by the Governing Board of the National Research Council, whose members are drawn from the councils of the National Academy of Sciences, National Academy of Engineering, and the Institute of Medicine. The members of the committee responsible for the report were chosen for their special competence, with regard for appropriate balance.

This report has been reviewed by a group other than the authors according to procedures approved by a Report Review Committee consisting of members of the National Academy of Sciences, the National Academy of Engineering, and the Institute of Medicine.

The National Academy of Sciences is a private, nonprofit, self-perpetuating society of distinguished scholars engaged in scientific and engineering research, dedicated to the furthering of science and technology and to their use for the general welfare. Upon the authority of the charter granted to it by the Congress in 1863, the Academy has a mandate that requires it to advise the federal government on scientific and technical matters. Dr. Frank Press is president of the National Academy of Sciences.

The National Academy of Engineering was established in 1964, under the charter of the National Academy of Sciences, as a parallel organization of outstanding engineers. It is autonomous in its administration and in the selection of its members, sharing with the National Academy of Sciences the responsibility for advising the federal government. The National Academy of Engineering also sponsors engineering programs aimed at meeting national needs, encourages education and research, and recognizes the superior achievements of engineers. Dr. Robert M. White is president of the National Academy of Engineering.

The Institute of Medicine was established in 1970 by the National Academy of Sciences to secure the services of eminent members of appropriate professions in the examination of policy matters pertaining to the health of the public. The Institute acts under the responsibility given to the National Academy of Sciences by its congressional charter to be an adviser to the federal government and, upon its own initiative, to identify issues of medical care, research, and education. Dr. Samuel O. Thier is president of the Institute of Medicine.

The National Research Council was organized by the National Academy of Sciences in 1916 to associate the broad community of science and technology with the Academy's purposes of furthering knowledge and advising the federal government. Functioning in accordance with general policies determined by the Academy, the Council has become the principal operating agency of both the National Academy of Sciences and the National Academy of Engineering in providing services to the government, the public, and the scientific and engineering communities. The Council is administered jointly by both academies and by the Institute of Medicine. Dr. Frank Press and Dr. Robert M. White are chairman and vice-chairman, respectively, of the National Research Council.

Support for this project was provided by the Federal Emergency Management Agency under Grant No. EMW-88-G-2786.

Library of Congress Catalog Card Number 89-13845
International Standard Book Number 0-309-04143-0

Copyright ©1990 by the National Academy of Sciences

Printed in the United States of America

333.917
N 277 m
1990

COMMITTEE ON COASTAL EROSION ZONE MANAGEMENT

WILLIAM L. WOOD, Purdue University, West Lafayette, Indiana,
  Chairman
ROBERT G. DEAN, University of Florida
MARTIN JANNERETH, Michigan Department of Natural
  Resources
JUDITH T. KILDOW, Massachusetts Institute of Technology
STEPHEN P. LEATHERMAN, University of Maryland
BERNARD LE MEHAUTE, University of Miami, Miami, Florida
DAVID W. OWENS, University of North Carolina, Chapel Hill
RUTHERFORD H. PLATT, University of Massachusetts
ROBERT L. WIEGEL, University of California, Berkeley

Consultant

GERALDINE BACHMAN, Marsolan Associates

Federal Agency Liaison Representatives

KATHRYN COUSINS, National Oceanic and Atmospheric
  Administration, Washington, D.C.
TODD L. WALTON, JR., U.S. Army Corps of Engineers Coastal
  Engineering Research Center, Vicksburg, Mississippi
S. JEFFRESS WILLIAMS, U.S. Geological Survey, Reston,
  Virginia

National Research Council Staff

SHEILA D. DAVID, Program Officer, Water Science and
  Technology Board
DONALD W. PERKINS, Associate Director, Marine Board
JEANNE AQUILINO, Project Secretary, Water Science and
  Technology Board

Federal Emergency Management Agency

MICHAEL BUCKLEY, Project Officer

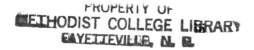
PROPERTY OF
METHODIST COLLEGE LIBRARY
FAYETTEVILLE, N. C.

Additional Resource Persons

JAMES H. BREED, Mobil Land Development Corporation
DON COLLINS, Federal Insurance Administration
ROBERT DOLAN, University of Virginia
GEORGE DOMURAT, Los Angeles District, Corps of Engineers
JOHN FLYNN, Ventura County Supervisor
JAMES McGRATH, California Coastal Commission
BRIAN MRAZIK, Federal Emergency Management Agency
WES OOMS, State Farm Insurance
FRANK REILLY, Federal Insurance Administration

WATER SCIENCE AND TECHNOLOGY BOARD

MICHAEL C. KAVANAUGH, James M. Montgomery Consulting Engineers, Oakland, California, *Chairman*
STEPHEN J. BURGES, University of Washington (through 6/30/89)
NORMAN H. BROOKS, California Institute of Technology
RICHARD A. CONWAY, Union Carbide Corporation, South Charleston, West Virginia
JAMES P. HEANEY, University of Florida
R. KEITH HIGGINSON, Idaho Department of Water Resources, Boise (through 6/30/89)
HOWARD C. KUNREUTHER, University of Pennsylvania
LUNA B. LEOPOLD, University of California, Berkeley (through 6/30/89)
G. RICHARD MARZOLF, Murray State University, Murray, Kentucky
ROBERT R. MEGLEN, University of Colorado at Denver
JAMES W. MERCER, GeoTrans, Herndon, Virginia (through 6/30/89)
DONALD J. O'CONNOR, Manhattan College, Bronx, New York
BETTY H. OLSON, University of California at Irvine
P. SURESH C. RAO, University of Florida
GORDON G. ROBECK, Consultant, Laguna Hills, California (through 6/30/89)
PATRICIA L. ROSENFIELD, The Carnegie Corporation of New York
DONALD D. RUNNELLS, University of Colorado, Boulder
A. DAN TARLOCK, Chicago Kent College Law School
HUGO F. THOMAS, Department of Environmental Protection, Hartford, Connecticut
JAMES R. WALLIS, IBM Watson Research Center, Yorktown Heights, New York
M. GORDON WOLMAN, The Johns Hopkins University, Baltimore, Maryland

Staff

STEPHEN D. PARKER, Director
SHEILA D. DAVID, Senior Staff Officer

CHRIS ELFRING, Senior Staff Officer
WENDY L. MELGIN, Staff Officer
JEANNE AQUILINO, Administrative Assistant
RENEE A. HAWKINS, Administrative Secretary
ANITA A. HALL, Senior Secretary

MARINE BOARD

SIDNEY A. WALLACE, Hill, Betts & Nash, Reston, Virginia, *Chairman*

BRIAN J. WATT, TECHSAVANT, Inc., Kingwood, Texas, *Vice Chairman*

ROGER D. ANDERSON, Cox's Wholesale Seafood, Inc., Tampa, Florida

ROBERT G. BEA, University of California, Berkeley, California

JAMES M. BROADUS III, Woods Hole Oceanographic Institution, Woods Hole, Massachusetts

F. PAT DUNN, Shell Oil Company, Houston, Texas

LARRY L. GENTRY, Lockheed Advanced Marine Systems, Sunnyvale, California

DANA R. KESTER, University of Rhode Island, Kingston, Rhode Island

JUDITH T. KILDOW, Massachusetts Institute of Technology, Cambridge, Massachusetts

WARREN LEBACK, Consultant, Princeton, New Jersey

BERNARD LE MEHAUTE, University of Miami, Miami, Florida

WILLIAM R. MURDEN, Murden Marine, Ltd., Alexandria, Virginia

EUGENE K. PENTIMONTI, American President Lines, Ltd., Oakland, California

JOSEPH D. PORRICELLI, ECO, Inc., Annapolis, Maryland

JERRY R. SCHUBEL, State University of New York, Stony Brook, New York

RICHARD J. SEYMOUR, Scripps Institution of Oceanography, La Jolla, California

ROBERT N. STEINER, Atlantic Container Line, South Plainfield, New Jersey

EDWARD WENK, JR., University of Washington, Seattle, Washington

Staff

CHARLES A. BOOKMAN, Director
DONALD W. PERKINS, Associate Director
SUSAN GARBINI, Project Officer
PAUL SCHOLZ, Sea Grant Fellow
ALEXANDER B. STAVOVY, Project Officer
WAYNE YOUNG, Project Officer

DORIS C. HOLMES, Staff Associate
AURORE BLECK, Senior Project Assistant
DELPHINE GLAZE, Senior Project Assistant
GLORIA B. GREEN, Project Assistant
CARLA D. MOORE, Project Assistant

Preface

In response to a request from the Federal Emergency Management Agency/Federal Insurance Administration (FEMA/FIA) in 1988, the National Research Council (NRC) established the Committee on Coastal Erosion Zone Management under the auspices of its Water Science and Technology Board and the Marine Board. The committee was asked to provide advice on appropriate erosion management strategies, supporting data needs, and applicable methodologies to administer these strategies through the National Flood Insurance Program.

The committee's task was a difficult one, owing to the complexity of the policy arena within which coastal erosion mitigation programs must be developed and to the uncertainty in trying to quantify coastal response to erosion-causing forces. An underlying concern of the committee in addressing its task was that of managing a valuable and complex natural resource. This concern was complicated by the fact that "value" exists in both the intrinsic natural attributes of the resource and in the material additions created by residency at the coast. The challenge was to create a balance in approaches to erosion mitigation in such a way as to provide opportunity for science and engineering to be used effectively in the planning and management process.

Congress has provided limited authorization for FEMA to implement a coastal erosion management program; however, this does not preclude the necessity for a broader public discussion of the appropriateness of such a program. The issue of whether the federal government should be involved in erosion insurance at all was of some concern within the committee. Several members were of the opinion that no federal insurance should be provided to those who take the risk of building (or buying) in an erosion zone and that those who do should bear their own losses. Further, one member believes that coastal erosion management programs and plans should be a function of state governments and not the federal government (see minority opinion, Appendix E). Conversely, some members argued in favor of a federal insurance program on coastal erosion that reflects the philosophy of the Upton-Jones Amendment (see page 3). Still others believe in the philosophies behind the Clean Water Act and the Coastal Zone Management Act where government participates in coastal protection but does not pay people for their losses.

The committee had to take into consideration a number of complicating and often conflicting factors. For example, federal, state, and local governmental structures create multijurisdictional overlaps that are often complicated by multistate and regional interests. Economic incentives to develop high-hazard, high-value coastal land often conflict with those interests wanting to preserve natural environments. The expenditure of tax dollars for erosion mitigation in coastal regions necessitates public representation through a government agency, which in turn may be viewed as an intrusion on private development. Additionally, coastal erosion often is caused by federal and local government actions, such as dredging and the building of dams on rivers supplying sand to the coast.

In an attempt to clarify broader coastal erosion zone management issues, this report goes beyond a simple, direct response to FEMA's requested tasks. This report does provide FEMA with the requested review and evaluation of existing federal and state erosion management programs, existing federal and state data collection programs and future needs, and engineering as well as policy alternatives to erosion mitigation and control. However, the committee wishes to point out that this report only provides guidelines for coastal erosion zone management. Many of the details and technical standards necessary to carry out the recommendations made in this report will require concentrated and detailed work by specialized groups of experts.

Toward the end of the committee's study, Hurricane Hugo caused major devastation and loss of coastal inland property in South Carolina. According to the Federal Insurance Administration, preliminary estimates for payment of all claims for flood damage resulting from Hurricane Hugo will be between $225 million and $275 million. At this time, the flood insurance fund, generated from premium income, is sufficient to pay this amount to compensate those insured who have suffered flood damage.

The committee was composed of an outstanding and diverse group of professionals, including two state coastal managers and professors of ocean policy, law, coastal geomorphology, policy, and coastal engineering. In its research, meetings, and writing for this report, the committee members gave generously and graciously of their expertise and time.

The committee wishes to acknowledge the outstanding support of the staffs of two NRC boards: the Water Science and Technology Board and the Marine Board. We appreciate their special contributions in the preparation of this report. Sheila David, Project Officer, and Jeanne Aquilino, Project Secretary of the Water Science and Technology Board, were instrumental in helping us meet our commitments in issuing this report. Don Perkins, Associate Director of the Marine Board, and Sheila David were extremely helpful with their suggestions and efforts in preparing and revising the draft reports.

Finally, I wish to personally extend my deepest appreciation to each of the committee members for their considerable attention to the complex task set before them. Their outstanding professional competence, patience, and cooperation deserve special recognition.

WILLIAM L. WOOD
Chairman

Contents

Executive Summary

Historically, coastal development in the United States was dominated by major urban regions oriented to commercial ports and defense installations. Elsewhere, coastal settlements were typically quiet fishing villages, vacation refuges, and older seaside resorts gradually evolving into year-round communities. Since the advent of the Interstate Highway System in the 1960s, increasing demand for coastal resources has expanded and transformed settlement patterns along accessible tidal and Great Lakes shorelines. Much of the U.S. population now lives within a two-hour drive of a coast and millions of inlanders travel much farther to spend vacations or transact business in coastal locations. Large numbers of retirees also have migrated coastward.

These population and economic pressures have transformed the lightly developed shorelines of earlier years into higher density resorts and urban complexes, for example, Ocean City, Maryland; Clearwater, Florida; Gulf Shores, Alabama; Galveston, Texas; and Newport Beach, California. In the process, conflicts arise between adjoining private owners, between units of political jurisdiction, between private and public rights on the shore, and between human activities and natural coastal processes, such as erosion.

The costs of shore erosion are varied and can be burdensome. Private homes, commercial structures, and government-owned buildings are undermined and sometimes destroyed if they are not

1

protected or relocated from a retreating shoreline. Public infrastructure (e.g., roads, sewers, water lines, parking lots, pavilions, toilets, bath houses) are similarly threatened by erosion. Shoreline engineering structures built to protect landward development from flooding and erosion themselves—if improperly designed, constructed, and maintained—can be undermined, overtopped, outflanked, or otherwise incapacitated by ongoing erosion. Beach erosion also exacerbates the vulnerability of coastal development to flood damage during hurricanes and other major storms.

Coastal erosion is a complex physical process involving many natural and human-induced factors. The natural factors include such variables as sand sources and sinks; changes in relative sea level or Great Lakes water levels; geological characteristics of the shore; sand size, density, and shape; sand-sharing system of beaches, dunes, and offshore bars; effects of waves, currents, tides, and wind; and the bathymetry of the offshore sea bottom. Human intervention alters these natural processes through such actions as the dredging of tidal entrances, construction of harbors in nearshore waters, construction of groins and jetties, hardening of shorelines with seawalls or revetments, construction of sediment-trapping upland dams, and beach nourishment.

The National Flood Insurance Program (NFIP) was established by the National Flood Insurance Act of 1968 as the primary federal program to reduce future flood costs to the nation. The NFIP provides insurance coverage for "damage and loss which may result from erosion and undermining of shorelines by waves or currents in lakes and other bodies of water exceeding anticipated cyclical levels." A fundamental goal of the NFIP is to be actuarially sound—namely, to cover all claims out of premium income and thereby reduce future dependence on federal tax money to subsidize the program. Since 1981 insurance premium rates have doubled, bringing the NFIP closer to being actuarially sound and self-supporting. Although NFIP insurance covers flood-related erosion losses, the Federal Emergency Management Agency (FEMA) has not yet exercised its legislative authority to identify flood-related erosion zones in coastal areas. Even though specific land management criteria for participating communities in flood-related erosion-prone areas were promulgated, they are inoperable without E-zone identification. However, several states and local governments have undertaken management programs to address erosion.

The Upton-Jones Amendment to the NFIP (P.L. 100-242, Sec-

tion 544; see Appendix A) adopts an approach that encourages retreat from eroding shorelines. Instead of insuring coastal structures
until they collapse, Section 544 authorizes advance payment of certain insurance benefits if the owner demolishes or relocates a structure "subject to imminent collapse or subsidence as a result of erosion
or undermining caused by waves or currents of water exceeding anticipated cyclical levels." Payment for demolition prior to collapse
would be 110 percent of the value of the structure (as defined in the
amendment). Payment for relocation would be the actual cost of
relocation up to 40 percent of the value of the structure.

The Upton-Jones Amendment represents an effort by Congress
to identify those structures most at risk from erosion and storm hazards and to encourage action to reduce losses prior to their total
destruction. So far the Upton-Jones Amendment has had only modest influence on the owners of property at risk from erosion. As of
August 1989, only 266 claims had been filed. This is modest in comparison with the total number of coastal structures threatened by
erosion. However, the committee believes it is too soon to evaluate
the true effectiveness of this amendment.

In 1988 FEMA's Federal Insurance Administration (FEMA/FIA)
asked the National Research Council (NRC) to provide advice on appropriate erosion management strategies, supporting data needs, and
applicable methodologies to administer these strategies through the
NFIP. Using the resources of both the Water Science and Technology
Board (WSTB) and the Marine Board, the NRC began this assessment of options for coastal erosion zone management. The study
reviews (1) existing and proposed NFIP legislative requirements relative to coastal erosion; (2) existing coastal erosion management
programs on the Great Lakes and the oceans surrounding the United
States, particularly those programs administered by the states, that
would be potentially applicable under the NFIP; (3) technical standards, methods, and data to support existing management programs
potentially applicable under the NFIP; and (4) the relationship between the structural and other alternatives for erosion control and
the land use management and zoning approach used under the NFIP.
Based on this review and the current state of knowledge of coastal
processes, the committee was asked to provide options for FEMA's
consideration to implement a coastal erosion zone management program.

Appendix B provides definitions of many terms used throughout
this report. The committee has provided its own definition of an E-

zone. The term "erosion," as used in this report, denotes the process
of wearing away of land by natural forces. It is not intended that
erosion imply loss due to flooding. However, as explained in Chapter
4, this is a gray area under the existing legislative guidelines.

In order to provide rational and defensible options, the committee believes it is necessary to evaluate and present information
on:

- natural shore processes,
- sources and sinks,
- environmental conditions,
- human-induced changes to the coast,
- examples of erosion and likely causes, and
- examples of erosion control and reasons for their success.

The study was carried out by the Committee on Coastal Erosion Zone Management over a 17-month period. The committee
included expertise in coastal engineering, geomorphology, geography, photogrammetry, sediment transport, law, policy, and land use
planning.

The first meeting was held in May 1988 when the committee was
briefed by FEMA/FIA officials on the nature and scope of the assigned task. At its second meeting held in July 1988, the committee
heard presentations on California's coastal erosion management program from representatives of the Corps of Engineers, the California
Coastal Commission, and a Ventura County supervisor. Additionally, two committee members briefed the committee on Great Lakes
states coastal erosion zone management programs. An outline for
the committee's report also was developed at this meeting.

At its third meeting, September 29-30, 1988, held in Florida,
the committee was briefed on Florida's coastal erosion management
programs. Viewpoints from the private insurance industry, private
developers, and the FIA were expressed by invited speakers. A brief
field trip was taken to the site of several successful beach nourishment
projects in Florida. The committee next met in March 1989 to draft
conclusions and recommendations for FEMA, and several members
of the committee met on May 8-9, 1989, in Washington, D.C., to
review and reorganize the report. A final committee meeting was
held on August 21-22, 1989, in Washington, D.C.

The Committee on Coastal Erosion Zone Management recognizes that the NFIP, through the requirement for minimum elevation
standards, has been successful in protecting structures located in

coastal areas prone to flooding and wave inundation. In the committee's view an erosion element of the NFIP should incorporate the following objectives:

1. Transfer economic costs of erosion losses from all federal taxpayers to the property owners at risk by charging premiums that approximate the risks of loss. The program should eventually become actuarial.

2. Discourage inappropriate development from occurring in erosion zones as delineated by FEMA or the states.

3. Promote the improvement of development and redevelopment practices in erosion-prone areas.

Pursuant to these objectives, the committee has reached the following conclusions and recommendations.

FEMA's Office of General Counsel has determined that certain of the following recommendations would require legislative action, particularly those concerned with erosion zone management and denial of NFIP coverage. This committee has not attempted to determine independently whether or not new legislation would be required for FEMA to implement any of these recommendations.

CONCLUSIONS AND RECOMMENDATIONS

Erosion Hazard Reduction

HAZARD DELINEATION

Conclusion

FEMA has not identified erosion hazard zones (E-zones) in implementing the NFIP. An accurate delineation of coastlines subject to erosion is essential to effective erosion and flood loss reduction and to an actuarially sound program.

Recommendations

• **In addition to flood depth, frequency, and velocity, FEMA's coastal hazard delineations should incorporate methodologies and data on erosion hazards.**

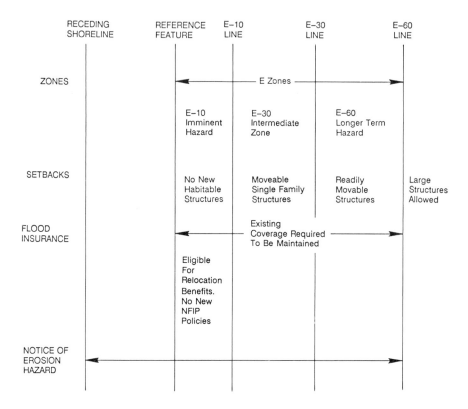

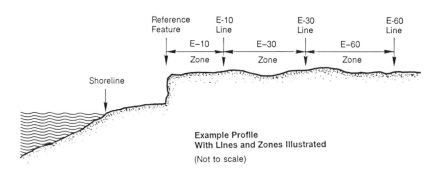

FIGURE E-1   Summary chart of E-lines and E-zones.

• FEMA should delineate coastlines subject to erosion (E-zones). These should include areas subject to imminent erosion hazards (within 10 years, E-10 zone), intermediate hazard (within 30 years, E-30 zone), and long-term hazard (within 60 years, E-60 zone) (see Figure E-1).

• The physical location of E-zones is dynamic. Therefore E-zone delineations should be based on a reference point (such as an erosion scarp, bluff, or vegetation line) that is a suitable indicator for determining E-zones. The location of this reference point moves as erosion takes place, and this fact must be incorporated in E-zone delineation.

RECOMMENDED METHODOLOGIES

Conclusion

FEMA's present methodology for determining shoreline recession rates should be improved to properly delineate E-zones. A historical shoreline change method would be least costly to implement. However, a more precise methodology based upon oceanographic data is preferable.

Recommendations

Thus, the committee recommends that FEMA:

• Utilize the historical shoreline change method to immediately begin mapping erosion hazard zones. FEMA should use existing acceptable shoreline change data and obtain additional erosion rate data to delineate E-zones for the NFIP. Care should be exercised in extrapolating erosion rate data owing to variable geologies and other factors; for example, the land may change from easily erodible sand to resistant material such as beach rock or vice versa.

• Further, the committee strongly urges that FEMA develop a preferred methodology based upon oceanographic data and statistical techniques. This methodology involves using available records of shoreline recession for analysis of the time history of oceanographic forces.

STANDARDS FOR DEVELOPMENT

Conclusion

Comprehensive management programs should be developed for all areas experiencing significant erosion.

However, a single uniform national "answer" to erosion problems is neither practical nor desirable. In addition, public planners and decision makers should avoid basing policies on stereotypes or preconceptions as to "typical" shorelines and their state of development and governance. Setbacks for new development, relocation of endangered structures, beach nourishment, and engineered shore protection structures or doing nothing may each be appropriate under specific localized conditions. In regard to the following recommendations, it is understood that if a program of coastal erosion control is implemented then E-zones shall be reassessed.

Recommendations

A. MINIMUM STANDARDS FOR STATE OR LOCAL MANAGE-
   MENT PROGRAMS

- No new development should be permitted seaward of the E-10 line, except coastal-dependent uses, such as piers and docks.
- Only readily movable structures should be permitted seaward of the E-60 line. Within this area, most development should be landward of the E-30 line, with states and local governments having the option of allowing variances for single family structures up to the E-10 line on preexisting lots that cannot meet an E-30 setback (see Figure E-1).
- New large structures in excess of 5,000 square feet (as in North Carolina) should not be allowed seaward of the E-60 line.
- FEMA should incorporate state setbacks that conform to or are more stringent than federal standards wherever possible.
- For new structures seaward of the E-60 line, pilings should be required (except on high bluffs) to be embedded to withstand a 100-year erosion event.
- While flexibility to address local needs should be retained, FEMA should establish minimum standards for local erosion management regulations. Coverage by state or local regulations that meet these minimum standards should be a prerequisite for community NFIP participation. Coverage by such a program also should be

a prerequisite for a property's eligibility for disaster relief and the community's eligibility for other federal programs, including recreation and open space funds, coastal management funds, highway and transportation funds, water and sewer funds, and beach nourishment projects other than those involved with the correction of human-induced erosion.

B. INSURANCE RATES AND AVAILABILITY

- No new NFIP policies should be issued for structures in delineated E-10 zones.
- NFIP policies for new structures in other E-zones should be actuarial.
- The portion of NFIP premiums that reflects erosion risk should decline with distance from the reference feature. This amount should be distinguished from that portion of the premium attributable to flood risk in annual NFIP billings to policy holders. (The purchase of flood insurance including the appropriate premium surcharge reflecting the erosion risk coverage should be mandatory for all buildings within the E-60 zone.)
- Communities should be encouraged through the proposed Community Rating System (CRS) to adopt stricter erosion zones—for example, E-50 for small structures and E-100 for large ones. Under the CRS, credits should be awarded toward reduced community-wide premium rates for adopting such stricter standards. For existing structures, lower premiums should be available if the buildings are retrofitted with pilings long enough to provide structural integrity and reduce the chance of structural failure.
- NFIP coverage should be maintained on eligible structures in the E-60 zone (excluding the E-10 zone) over the life of any federally related financing, including secondary mortgage market transfers.
- NFIP should establish insurance rates based on anticipated relocation benefits of 40 percent of the structure's value (as determined under Section 544).

C. SECTION 544 (UPTON-JONES) RELOCATION AND DEMOLITION BENEFITS

- FEMA should define E-10 zones as being subject to "imminent threat of collapse due to erosion" and therefore eligible for benefits under Section 544.

- Owners of structures in danger of imminent collapse (E-10 zones) should be notified of levels of risk and availability of Section 544 benefits.

- Two years after such notification, NFIP premiums on structures remaining in an E-10 zone should be increased substantially. Alternatively, coverage may be frozen at 40 percent of the current value of the structure (equivalent to maximum payable for a "proper relocation" under Section 544).

- No Section 544 relocation payment should be made if any part of the structure remains seaward of the E-30 zone (E-60 for large structures) after relocation.

- Sites vacated by demolition or relocation funded by Section 544 should be covered by deed restrictions prohibiting future redevelopment involving an enclosed structure.

- Relocation should be encouraged over demolition for purposes of Section 544. Demolition should be employed only where
    a. relocation is technically unfeasible;
    b. there is no feasible site beyond the E-30 or E-60 line where the structure may be economically relocated;
    c. the structure poses an imminent danger to the public safety in its E-10 location; or
    d. demolition would be less expensive than relocation.

- An appeal procedure should be established by FEMA whereby aggrieved property owners may challenge a presumption that erosion is continuing at the estimated rate.

IMPACTS OF NAVIGATIONAL AND FLOOD CONTROL PROJECTS ON SHORE STABILITY

Conclusion

Jettied entrances and breakwaters forming harbors along sandy coasts often cause accretion updrift and erosion downdrift of the project. Up-river deforestation can cause erosion of banks and deposition at the river estuary and along the coast. Additionally, when rivers that deliver sand and sediment to the coast are dammed for flood control and other purposes, beach erosion can result over the long term.

Recommendations

• Sand dredged from entrances and harbors, if of beach quality, can be used effectively to enhance beach nourishment. However, much of this resource has been deposited offshore and lost to the littoral system. A national policy should be adopted that requires placement of good-quality sand, dredged from harbors and entrances, as beach nourishment.

• Procedures should be developed, as a part of the environmental impact statement process, to evaluate the erosion potential and costs of navigation structures such as jetties and breakwaters. Studies should be made on advisability and means of shifting the cost of erosion from downdrift property owners (public and private) to the sponsors of the projects responsible for erosion.

• Studies should be conducted to develop recommendations on a proper procedure to mitigate negative effects of existing and planned structures that cause adverse effects on the adjacent property owners. Examples are sand bypassing coastal structures and beach nourishment using sand sources other than sand bypassing.

• Planners and decision makers should consider the effects of dams and flow regulation upon the supply of sand to beaches.

EROSION CONTROL THROUGH COASTAL ENGINEERING

Conclusion

There are many examples of properly planned, designed, constructed, and maintained seawalls and revetments that have prevented further retreat of the shoreline, but beaches sometimes have been lost as a result. There are also examples of properly planned, designed, constructed, and maintained detached breakwaters and groin fields that have been effective in the local control of coastal erosion; however, impacts on downdrift beaches must be considered. Beach nourishment is now the method of choice for beach preservation in many coastal communities. While some beach fill projects are performing well (e.g., Miami Beach, Florida), there is little monitoring of these projects, which is necessary for long-term evaluation.

Recommendations

• The use of properly engineered structures should be permitted in regions where they are physically and economically justified and consistent with state and local programs and where possible adverse impacts are properly evaluated.

• The main purposes of beach nourishment are to provide beaches for recreational use and as storm buffers for shore development. A secondary benefit is coastal erosion control. Investigations should be made of the economics of transporting sand by bulk carriers from relatively distant sources to densely used coastal areas where the value of beaches is great and coastal erosion control is amenable to this approach of beach nourishment.

SAND AND GRAVEL MINING

Conclusion

Sand and gravel mined from beaches and riverbeds near the coast can result in beach erosion.

Recommendations

• Procedures should be developed, as a part of the environmental impact statement process, to evaluate the erosion potential and costs of sand and gravel mining.

• Policies should be developed to shift the cost of erosion resulting from mining sand and gravel from downdrift property owners to those responsible for the mining operations.

SUBSIDENCE

Conclusion

Many coastal regions have subsided owing to both natural and human-induced causes. This has resulted in coastal erosion in some areas.

Recommendations

• Procedures should be developed, as a part of the environmental impact statement process, to evaluate the subsidence caused by removal of subsurface fluids and to evaluate the erosion potential and costs. Studies should be made on determination of cause and means of shifting the costs of erosion to those responsible for the erosion from those affected by the erosion.

• Methods of mitigating erosion-causing subsidence should be improved, where possible, and implemented where economically feasible.

Education

Conclusion

The current state of public education about coastal erosion, the causes of coastal erosion, its long-term impacts, and the possible responses to it is inadequate. A more informed or educated public (including buyers, sellers, developers, planners, engineers, and public officials) would be able to make better long-term coastal development decisions.

Recommendations

• A public education program carried out at the national, state, and local levels should be an integral part of the national policy on coastal erosion. FEMA should strive to inform the general public of the risks associated with development in the coastal zone.

• Methods should be established by FEMA to provide effective and regular notice to all land owners in E-zones as to the existence and magnitude of erosion (e.g., through notations on annual flood insurance premium notices, notations on deeds or otherwise included in the property's claim of title).

Data Base Development and Research

Conclusion

Available data and methodologies are adequate for FEMA to develop an interim erosion insurance element for the NFIP. However, better knowledge and understanding of processes and a better data base are necessary for a long-term, risk-quantified (based) program and should be developed and incorporated into the NFIP as soon as available.

Recommendations

- FEMA should develop a shoreline change data base for use in implementing a national erosion insurance element of the NFIP. This data base must incorporate the local character of spatial and temporal shoreline changes, properly evaluating the impact of major coastal storms and shore engineering projects on the erosional trend. The level of detail required should be commensurate with local land use change.

- Unevaluated shoreline data exist for the U.S. coasts, but considerable analytical effort would be necessary to develop these data into a readily applied, reliable, and consistent form. FEMA should develop standards, based on a technical analysis, that can be applied to developing a national data base in an appropriate form. Florida and New Jersey have established such a data base and may serve as models for FEMA's data acquisition program.

- Ultimately, FEMA should use a statistical method for modeling erosion rates; however, presently the necessary data are not available.

RESEARCH

Conclusion

The state of the art in predicting erosion rates is poor and is technically difficult without both general and site-specific research. The ability to predict erosion and coastal change is fundamental to coastal management, environmental decision making, and shoreline preservation.

Recommendation

- FEMA should actively support efforts to develop research on defining long-term statistical oceanographic climate, particularly the wave climate, shore processes near tidal inlets, and coastal response to storms and hurricanes. FEMA should also encourage the U.S. Army Corps of Engineers, the National Oceanic and Atmospheric Administration (NOAA), and other appropriate agencies to conduct research on the effect of engineering structures (seawalls, revetments, groins, detached structures), beach nourishment, and dredging operations on coastal erosion.

Unified National Program for Floodplain Management

Conclusion

The Unified National Program for Floodplain Management (March 1986) in its current form lacks any component to address erosion. It contains no explicit discussion of erosion as a contributing factor in coastal flood losses. If suitably revised, it could serve as the fundamental expression of a national policy on coastal erosion.

Recommendations

• FEMA should revise the Unified National Program for Floodplain Management to reflect federal policies and programs concerning erosion zone management.

• FEMA should convene a national Task Force on Coastal Erosion Zone Management. This body would include experts from universities and federal agencies having policy or program responsibilities affecting coastal erosion. Experts from states with critical erosion problems and/or significant coastal erosion management programs also should be invited to participate. The purposes of the Task Force would include:

a. assisting FEMA in developing and promulgating nationwide standards for erosion hazard reduction equivalent to the 100-year flood standard;

b. reviewing internal procedures of participating agencies to determine compatibility with erosion management provisions of the Unified National Program (as revised);

c. reviewing the applicability of Executive Orders 11988 and 11990 to the management of E-Zones and, if appropriate, recommend revisions to the President; and

d. serve as an ongoing technical advisory committee concerning coastal erosion with the capability of commissioning special studies and research projects where appropriate to further goals of the Unified National Program.

1

Introduction and Background

Thirty of the nation's fifty states have coastlines on the Atlantic and Pacific Oceans, the Gulf of Mexico, and the Great Lakes. These 30 states contain approximately 85 percent of the nation's population, with nearly 53 percent of this population living in a 50-mile-wide corridor bordering the coast. Projections to the end of this century indicate continued population growth within this coastal corridor, accompanied by an increasing demand for shoreline development. At present, there is considerable public concern over coastal erosion, coastal erosion control measures, and coastal land use regulations and preservation of a natural coastline.

Unlike flooding, there is no well-defined federal program designed to mitigate property damage or loss caused by coastal erosion. Coastal erosion mitigation programs must be formulated in a complex policy arena in which federal, state, county, and municipal governments share jurisdictions over the coast. Consequently, each length of coast is subject to multiple layers of public authority. Likewise, public participants (e.g., residential, industrial, commercial, preservational, or recreational) reflect another diverse set of interests in the coast.

Development of a coastal erosion mitigation program is complicated by a number of existing conditions. First, the capability to predict coastal response to erosion-causing forces in the environment is imprecise. Second, the ability to predict erosion-causing forces is not well developed and not likely to be perfected. Third, private erosion insurance essentially is unavailable on property built close (hundreds of feet) to an eroding shore.

Erosion mitigation problems also involve the issue of cost to the public. This cost includes data acquisition and administration of an erosion management program, to say nothing of the intangible costs of the loss of beach usage. Consideration also must be given to the resources available to offset these costs. In many cases, the least costly solution to coastal erosion problems is to improve sand management practices that adversely affect shoreline stability. As examples, good-quality sand dredged from channel entrances should be placed on the adjacent beaches, and sand mining from certain riverbeds near coastlines should be discontinued.

The Committee Report for the Upton-Jones legislation encourages FEMA to participate in the task of developing a coastal erosion management program. This specific piece of legislation addresses problems of those states presently suffering significant erosion along their coasts. Opinions differ as to (1) whether this is an appropriate activity for the federal government, (2) whether it properly falls within the rubric of "insurance," and (3) whether this is the best way to address the problems of shore protection.

In response to the Upton-Jones legislation, some observers might argue for a laissez-faire philosophy that opts for no government involvement. This attitude presumes that those who take the risk of owning shorefront property and reap the benefits of living along the coast will respond to the marketplace or their emotions but that these individuals should make their own decisions about remaining in a potentially hazardous position. Such observers might argue further that the government should have no role in either prescribing land use or protecting those who choose to take risks.

Other observers might argue in favor of a regulatory philosophy that encourages state government to manage the coast. A state program might in the long run provide a cost saving for the United States. However, the Upton-Jones legislation does provide a carrot, to those who would build or live in erosion-prone areas, to depart and let the natural systems take their course.

Regardless of reaction to the existing Upton-Jones legislation, there are several types of policy goals that should be reflected in any effort by FEMA to formulate a more comprehensive national policy on erosion. First, certain goals are implicit to the National Flood Insurance Act providing FEMA's basic authority to engage in flood-related erosion mitigation:

• Reduce the costs, both monetary and nonmonetary, inflicted by erosion on public and private investment in coastal areas.

• Reallocate the costs of erosion-related losses (including flood damage) from all federal taxpayers to the population of persons owning structures in flood- or erosion-prone areas through the mechanism of actuarial insurance premiums.

• Promote better shoreline management to achieve multiple goals in addition to flood/erosion hazard reduction (e.g., shoreline access, water quality improvement, public recreation, and preservation or restoration of natural ecosystems).

A second set of goals relates to the nature of erosion as a physical process:

• Provide flexibility in a national policy to accommodate regional variations stemming from differing shoreline types, erosion rates, settlement patterns, political structures, and extent of human-induced intervention in coastal processes (see Chapter 3).

• Initiate action to eliminate human-induced erosion.

• Accommodate seasonal and other temporal variation in the incidence of erosion losses (e.g., in the irregular cycles of high and low levels of the Great Lakes).

A third set of goals relates to fairness and administrative feasibility:

• Facilitate efficient administration through clarity of requirements and presentation of erosion rate data on Federal Insurance Rate Maps (FIRMs).

• Avoid redundant federal studies by using existing state or local erosion rate data, maps, and enforcement mechanisms whenever feasible.

• Afford opportunity for the affected public to participate in the regulatory process, including right of appeal.

• Place the decision-making process as close as possible to the affected property owner pursuant to national standards.

• Promote consistency with other related federal programs (e.g., Coastal Zone Management, Clean Water Act, shore protection programs, etc.).

This report has been assembled with a multidisciplinary perspective. It expresses a consensus strengthened by the diversity of backgrounds and philosophies of the individual committee members.

It has drawn on the experience from existing management programs; individuals at the local, state, and federal levels; and private sector interests in the coastal zone. The committee's intent in preparing this report is to provide direction to the federal government and its agencies and at the same time to provide a document to assist all members of the coastal community.

2
Coastal Erosion:
Its Causes, Effects, and Distribution

INTRODUCTION

This chapter discusses how beaches are formed and factors that determine coastal erosion, stability, or accretion. It also contains a summary of U.S. coastline characteristics, which serves to emphasize the diversity of shore types that must be considered in erosion management policies.

Historical shoreline changes along the coasts of the United States range from highly erosional to accretional. Superimposed on these long-term trends, however, can be rapid, extreme erosion caused by coastal storms from which the shore may or may not recover. In addition, the high likelihood of significant increases in sea level also has the potential to affect future shore erosion trends (National Research Council, 1987a).

A quantitative understanding of these short- and long-term shoreline changes is essential for the establishment of rational policies to regulate development in the coastal zone. Shoreline changes can be due to natural causes or they can be human-induced. Several common causes of human-induced shoreline change are

- construction or modification of inlets for navigational purposes,
- construction of harbors with breakwaters built in nearshore regions,

- construction of dams on rivers with steep gradients,
- sand mining from riverbeds in the near coastal area, and
- extraction of ground fluids resulting in coastal subsidence.

The human-induced causes are particularly relevant for policy makers to consider.

Beaches can change on various time scales from short-duration, dramatic changes to slow, almost imperceptible evolution that over time yields significant displacements. An important part of the FEMA program implementation is determination of the long-term trend of shoreline change. Unfortunately, storm-induced short-term beach variations can be so large that they may mask long-term trends. Another complicating factor is that at some locations the shoreline change trend rate itself has changed during the past several decades; quite often these changes are human-induced. Table 2-1 summarizes the possible natural contributions to shoreline change.

REGIONAL VARIATION

Types of Beaches

The United States has three general types of beaches: pocket, mainland, and barrier beaches. Beaches are composed of loose sediment particles, ranging in grain size from fine sand to large cobbles. Pocket beaches form between erosion-resistant headlands and are usually quite small. Pocket beaches are common along the rocky coast of New England and the cliffed coasts of California and Oregon. Because the sediment that constitutes pocket beaches is trapped by adjacent headlands, these beaches respond to prevailing waves; there is little movement of littoral sediment to or from adjacent beaches.

Mainland (also called strandplain) beaches are the most common type along the Pacific coast and on the Great Lakes, where the adjacent bluffs often are over 100 feet high. These beaches develop anywhere that ample sediment supply allows for accumulation along the shoreline. The beach usually is derived from the adjacent erodible cliff material. Mainland beaches backed by high eroding bluffs are well displayed along outer Cape Cod, Massachusetts. Elsewhere, mainland beaches can be quite low, such as those found in northern New Jersey and Delaware and along parts of the Gulf coastal plain. The mainland beaches of Holly Beach, Louisiana, are particularly low lying and susceptible to storm flooding.

TABLE 2-1 Summary of Natural Factors Affecting Shoreline Change

Factor	Effect	Time Scale	Comments
Sediment supply (sources and sinks)	Accretion/erosion	Decades to millennia	Natural supply from inland (e.g., river floods, cliff erosion) or shoreface and inner shelf sources can contribute to shoreline stability or accretion
Sea level rise	Erosion	Centuries to millennia	Relative sea level rise, including effects of land subsidence, is important
Sea level change	Erosion (for increases in sea level)	Months to years	Causes poorly understood, interannual variations that may exceed 40 years of trend (e.g., El Niño)
Storm surge	Erosion	Hours to days	Very critical to erosion magnitude
Large wave height	Erosion	Hours to months	Individual storms or seasonal effects
Short wave period	Erosion	Hours to months	Individual storms or seasonal effects
Waves of small steepness	Accretion	Hours to months	Summer conditions
Alongshore currents	Accretion, no change, or erosion	Hours to millennia	Discontinuities (updrift ≠ downdrift) and nodal points
Rip currents	Erosion	Hours to months	Narrow seaward-flowing currents that may transport significant quantities of sediment offshore
Underflow	Erosion	Hours to days	Seaward-flowing, near-bottom currents may transport significant quantities of sediment during coastal storms
Inlet presence	Net erosion; high instability	Years to centuries	Inlet-adjacent shorelines tend to be unstable because of fluctuations or migration in inlet position; net effect of inlets is erosional owing to sand storage in tidal shoals
Overwash	Erosional	Hours to days	High tides and waves cause sand transport over barrier beaches
Wind	Erosional	Hours to centuries	Sand blown inland from beach
Subsidence Compaction	Erosion	Years to millennia	Natural or human-induced withdrawal of subsurface fluids
Tectonic	Erosion/accretion	Instantaneous	Earthquakes
	Erosion/accretion	Centuries to millennia	Elevation or subsidence of plates

Slope instability is a major concern along erodible mainland coasts. Slope instability is largely controlled by the local geology, water level, wave action, and ground water movement. Bluff failure, concomitant loss of land, and sometimes houses are a continual problem along outer Cape Cod (Leatherman, 1987), the western shore of the Chesapeake Bay (Leatherman, 1986), and parts of the California coast (e.g., San Diego and Los Angeles county beaches). Extreme instability problems occur along the Great Lakes, where nearly 65 percent of the 16,047-kilometer-long shoreline is designated as having significant erosion (Edil, 1982).

Barrier beaches are perhaps the most dynamic coastal land masses along the open-ocean coast. These land forms predominate the U.S. East and Gulf coasts from Long Island, New York, to Texas. Barrier beaches can extend continuously for 10 to 100 miles, interrupted only by tidal inlets. Physically separated barrier islands often are linked by the longshore sediment transport system, so that an engineering action taken in any one beach area can have major impacts on adjacent downdrift beaches. For example, the south shore of Long Island, New York, is considered a single littoral cell. The eroding headlands and mainland beaches at Montauk Point to the east supply a portion of the sand that moves westward along the barrier beach chain (Southampton/Westhampton beaches, Fire Island, Jones Beach, the Rockaways) and is eventually deposited in New York harbor (Leatherman, 1985). Barrier islands are typically low lying, flood prone, and underlain by easily erodible, unconsolidated sediments. Thus, these land forms are especially difficult to develop because they are so dynamic.

BEACH PROCESSES—THE NATURAL SYSTEM

Natural beaches are formed by the accumulation of loose sediment, primarily sand, along the U.S. coasts. Their morphology is the result of antecedent conditions and sediment supply as well as the forces of waves, tides, currents, and winds. Beaches respond to changes in these forces and conditions on time scales ranging from hours to millennia. A discussion of the formation and processes of beach change follows.

Beach Sands: Sources and Sinks

Beaches are formed by an accumulation of sediment at the shoreline. The factors that determine coastal change are the rate of rise or fall in sea level relative to the land, the frequency and severity of storms, and the total volume of sand size and coarser sediments available in the sand-sharing system. Many coastal regions can be segmented into compartments; the boundaries are defined by the geologic features and processes that isolate the transport of littoral sediments from adjacent coastal compartments. Each compartment normally is composed of one or more sand sources and sand sinks, and the beach and nearshore serve as a conduit for the flow of sand between the sources and sinks.

Many factors are involved in the natural processes that provide sandy sediment to the coast. Often, the sand sources are local and transport distances are short; however, sometimes sediments are carried great distances before deposition occurs. There are five general sources of beach sediment: (1) terrestrial, (2) headlands, (3) shoreface, (4) biogenic production, and (5) the inner shelf. Their contributions vary with geographic location.

Terrestrial erosion and runoff provide rivers with large quantities of sediment of widely varying grain size and composition. These coarse-grained sediments then are carried toward the coast and may eventually reach the shore and be dispersed to adjacent beaches by littoral transport processes. However, to be significant sources of sand, rivers must have fairly high gradients. Many rivers along the U.S. Pacific coast were major contributors of sand, but dam building has greatly reduced the sediment that reaches the beaches. In contrast, most rivers along the Atlantic and Gulf coastal plains have low gradients and limited capacities to transport coarse sediment. Nearly all of the sand entering these rivers and transported seaward is deposited in their flood plains or estuaries and never reaches the open-coast beaches; the Mississippi River in Louisiana is an obvious exception.

Headland and linear bluff areas along coasts offer another major source of beach sand; wave undercutting and slumping make available large volumes of sediment for redistribution by wave action. Sand-size and coarser materials are carried by longshore currents along the beach, while the finer silts and clays are transported seaward into deep water. These finer materials also may be deposited in backbarrier lagoons if inlets are present.

The shoreface (i.e., the subaqueous portion of a beach) is another source of coastal sediment. Wave action erodes sand from a beach and shoreface, and longshore currents transport it downdrift. In this manner sand is recycled continually as the shore retreats.

Calcium carbonate (CaCO₃, such as found in shells) accounts for much of the beach sand in lower latitude tropical and subtropical regions and can contribute to beaches in middle- and even high-latitude areas as well. In most cases the shell debris is provided by organisms living in shallow areas close to the beach. The majority of carbonate particles are derived from disintegration of calcareous hard parts of invertebrate fauna such as molluscs, brachipods, corals, echinoderms, and foraminifera. Some beaches, however, also contain significant contributions of shell derived from older estuarine or lagoonal deposits that crop out and are eroded along the shoreface.

The inner shelf offshore of wide and gently sloping coastal plains also can be an important source of beach materials where there is an abundance of relict sand on the sea bottom. During the gradual rise in sea level over the past 15,000 years since glacial times, marine sand bodies have been eroded and the sediment redistributed by coastal currents. Over the long term, sand may be moved landward across the shelf where it can be incorporated eventually into the littoral system.

In contrast to sediment sources, littoral sinks function to reduce the volume of sand along the coast. The most common sinks to beaches are landward transport of sand through tidal inlets to form flood-tide shoals, storm-generated overwash deposits, landward-migrating sand dunes, losses down submarine canyons that extend close to shore (Pacific coast only), losses from sediment abrasion (largely the CaCO₃ fraction), and losses from human-induced causes such as mining, dredging, and breakwaters and jetties (Dolan et al., 1987).

Seasonal Fluctuations

Beaches respond quickly to changing wave conditions. In particular, steep (i.e., storm) waves formed by a combination of large wave heights and short wave periods tend to result in seaward sediment transport and shoreline recession. Thus, stormy winter (and hurricane) waves generally cause erosion, whereas milder and longer period summer waves promote beach recovery. Thus, beach width fluctuates on a seasonal basis for many U.S. beaches. These natural, interannual changes in shoreline position should not be confused with net long-term changes. Relatively poor documentation exists to quantify seasonal beach changes around the U.S. coastline; beach width may fluctuate by 100 feet or more (Johnson, 1971), but the national average is probably about half of this amount.

Storm-Related Beach Changes

Storm surges also contribute substantially to the beach erosion process. These above-normal tides are caused primarily by the high winds (i.e., shoreward-directed wind stress) and the reduced barometric pressures associated with major tropical or extratropical (i.e., low pressure) storms. Along the Atlantic and Gulf coast shorelines, the 100-year return period storm surges are approximately 12 to 15 feet above mean sea level. The 100-year storm surges along the Pacific shore are much smaller because of the narrow continental shelf. The largest documented storm surge along the U.S. coast was caused by Hurricane Camille in 1969, when the water was elevated 22.4 feet above normal at Pass Christian, Mississippi.

The three most important factors contributing to beach and dune erosion during storms are (1) storm surge heights, (2) storm surge duration, and (3) wave steepness (ratio of wave height to length). Almost all hurricane-induced erosion is limited because the time scale of the erosion process is shorter than the duration of the near-peak storm tides. Therefore, only a percent of the potential erosion actually may be realized. "Northeasters" (i.e., severe storms coming from the northeast along the Atlantic Coast) can last for days and therefore can achieve their full erosional potential.

Trends of Shoreline Change

The long-term trends of shoreline change depend on a number of factors, and all the causative processes cannot be quantified at present. Relevant factors include the antecedent topography (geomorphology) and the geologic rise of sea level, which has caused the shoreline to shift landward across the present-day continental shelf during the last 15,000 years. In some areas submerged sand on the inner shelf still is being transported shoreward and thus contributes to overall shoreline stability or accretion (Williams and Meisburger, 1987). In other areas there are no offshore sources of sand, and the slowly rising sea level induces beach erosion. Local land subsidence caused by natural or human-induced processes also can cause shoreline recession. Finally, the equilibrium beach profile is not well established along some (particularly glaciated) coasts, and sand is transported seaward for this reason alone even if there are no other causes.

Beach stability also must be considered in terms of alongshore discontinuities, which can cause areas of long-term erosion (e.g., headlands) to be in close proximity to areas of long-term accretion (e.g., sand spits). For example, headland erosion along the outer Cape Cod shoreline supplies the sand necessary for the continued accretion of Provincetown spit (Leatherman, 1987). Elsewhere, erosion may be pervasive on one flank of a coastal land form, such as the severe erosion on the northern section at Cape Hatteras, North Carolina, while the adjacent southern flank experiences long-term accretion.

Because of these complexities, the only reliable basis at present for determining long-term shoreline changes or stability is through analysis of site-specific data. The methods of obtaining such data are described in Chapter 6.

Natural Subsidence

Numerous examples of naturally occurring subsidence can be seen around the nation. For example, in the Mississippi River delta the weight of the accumulating sediment causes continued compaction and sinking. Earthquakes can result in rapid downward displacement of the land surface. An example of this type of tectonic subsidence occurred during the 1964 earthquake at Homer Spit, Alaska. This severe earthquake caused differential subsidence amounting to about 3 feet near the headland attachment and nearly 7 feet at the tip of the spit (Smith et al., 1985).

Subsidence usually results in a similar impact on the shore: beach erosion. When nearshore elevations drop, it is equivalent to a sea level rise of the same magnitude; the beach profile is thrown out of equilibrium by the creation of a sand sink offshore, and this induces offshore sediment transport and shore recession.

Stinson Beach, north of San Francisco, California, demonstrates that beach erosion does not always follow land subsidence if ample sand supplies are available from other sources. During the 1906 earthquake, the land dropped as much as 1 foot and moved 13.5 feet horizontally (Ritter, 1969). Residents reported that waves overtopped the spit far more frequently after the earthquake than before, but because adequate quantities of sand are supplied from contiguous regions, the spit is relatively stable on average.

Beach erosion at Stinson Beach was severe during the winter of 1982/1983 because of a series of large storms, several of which occurred when tides were abnormally high (i.e., spring tides). El Niño also contributed to high water conditions. Near the end of

FIGURE 2-1 Several homes in jeopardy and vertical scarp, western end of Seadrift, Stinson Beach, California, January 27, 1983. SOURCE: Photo provided by Robert E. Wiegel.

FIGURE 2-2 Riprap largely covered by accretion of sand, Seadrift, Stinson Beach, California, November 15, 1987. SOURCE: Photo provided by Robert E. Wiegel.

January 1983, several homes were nearly lost (Figure 2-1), and an emergency-engineered seawall was built. The beach has gradually recovered, and much of the quarry-rock seawall has been covered naturally by sand (Figure 2-2). This example further illustrates the dynamic nature of the beach, which varies on a daily, monthly, and yearly basis.

HUMAN-INDUCED CHANGES

Inlets, Jetties, and Dredged Entrances

Natural channel entrances have a substantial capacity to modify sediment transport in their vicinity. However, artificially dredged channel entrances, structurally modified for navigational purposes, have a much greater potential for affecting the adjacent shores. These impacts can have a different magnitude depending on the characteristics of the particular entrance (Table 2-2). Effects can extend miles from the entrance and are greatest where there is substantial net longshore sediment transport. The following three examples illustrate how human-induced changes affect beaches.

OCEAN CITY INLET, MARYLAND

The barrier island breach that later became Ocean City Inlet was caused by a major hurricane in September 1933. The inlet was stabilized by jetties soon after the breach occurred. Net longshore sediment transport is toward the south and estimated at 140,000 m³/year. No sustained effort has been made to carry out a sand-bypassing program. The impacts on the adjacent shoreline have been substantial: the immediate downdrift (i.e., south) shoreline has migrated landward a distance equal to the complete width of the barrier island in the last 50 years (Leatherman, 1984). Figure 2-3 shows changes in the Ocean City shoreline from 1931 to 1972 and presents a sediment budget for the area. All of the factors listed in Table 2-2 have contributed to these changes, with the exception of dredge disposal in deep water.

ST. MARY'S ENTRANCE, FLORIDA

The natural river entrance at St. Mary's was stabilized by jetty construction between 1881 and 1902. The jetties, which are low and permeable, allow flood waters to flow over them into the inlet.

TABLE 2-2 Mechanisms by Which Modified Inlets Can Affect the Sediment
Budget of Adjacent Shorelines

Mechanism	Net Deficit to Adjacent Shorelines?
1. Storage against updrift jetties	No, balanced by downdrift erosion
2. Ebb tidal shoal growth	Generally
3. Flood tidal shoal growth	Yes
4. Dredge disposal in deep water	Yes (very large sand quantities have already been permanently lost)
5. Leaky jetties	Yes

SOURCE: Modified from Dean, 1989.

During ebb flow the ocean tide is low, and the seaward-directed
flow is confined between the jetties. As a result, there has been a
major alteration of the ebb tidal shoals, which are large depositional
features formed seaward of the inlet by sand transport of the ebb tidal
currents. A total of 90 million cubic meters of sand was removed from
the nearshore and displaced farther offshore in the ebb tidal shoals
(Olsen, 1977).

PORT CANAVERAL, FLORIDA

This inlet was cut in 1951, the jetties were constructed in 1953
and 1954, and a beach nourishment project was carried out in 1974.
The net longshore sediment transport has been estimated by the U.S.
Army Corps of Engineers (1967) to be 270,000 m^3/year toward the
south. Results of shoreline change rates over the periods 1877-1951
(long term before entrance), 1955-1987 (postentrance establishment
to prenourishment), and 1974-1986 (postnourishment) are presented
in Figure 2-4. Primary impacts include interruption of the longshore
sediment transport, impoundment of the north jetty to capacity, and
offshore disposal of maintenance dredging material.

Sand Disposal Offshore

Disposal of beach-quality dredged sand offshore often results in
a significant adverse impact on adjacent shorelines. The primary
erosional effects occur on the downdrift shoreline, but erosion also

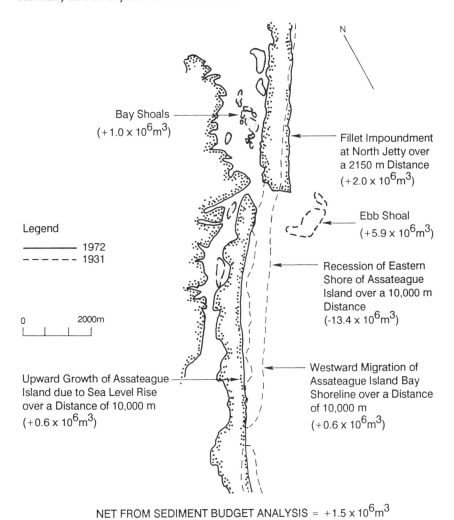

Bay Shoals
$(+1.0 \times 10^6 m^3)$

Fillet Impoundment
at North Jetty over
a 2150 m Distance
$(+2.0 \times 10^6 m^3)$

Ebb Shoal
$(+5.9 \times 10^6 m^3)$

Legend

——————— 1972
— — — — — 1931

Recession of Eastern
Shore of Assateague
Island over a 10,000 m
Distance
$(-13.4 \times 10^6 m^3)$

0   2000m

Upward Growth of Assateague
Island due to Sea Level Rise
over a Distance of 10,000 m
$(+0.6 \times 10^6 m^3)$

Westward Migration of
Assateague Island Bay
Shoreline over a Distance
of 10,000 m
$(+0.6 \times 10^6 m^3)$

NET FROM SEDIMENT BUDGET ANALYSIS = $+1.5 \times 10^6 m^3$

FIGURE 2-3 Components of sediment budget analysis, Ocean City, Maryland.
SOURCE: Dean and Perlin, 1977.

can occur on the updrift shoreline if jetties are not present or are
leaky. The beaches and nearshore system in the vicinity of a natural
tidal entrance to a bay can be considered as a "sand-sharing system,"
and the ebb tidal shoal is a vital part of this system. If a portion
of this ebb tidal shoal is lowered by dredging, a sand sink is created
and the remainder of the system responds by providing sand from

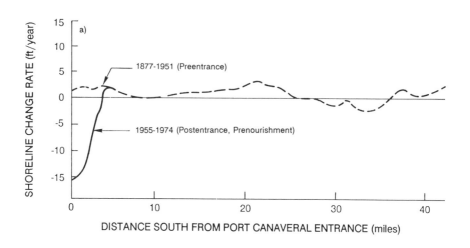

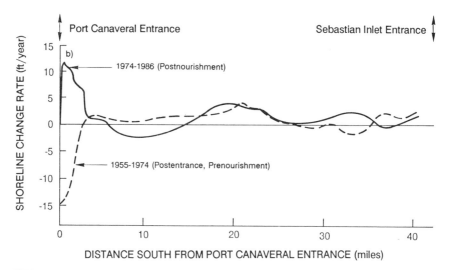

FIGURE 2-4 Effects of establishment of Port Canaveral, Florida, entrance and subsequent nourishment project on downdrift beaches. Top: Effects of channel entrance on downdrift beach stability, compared to preentrance condition. Bottom: Shoreline changes following 1974 nourishment project. SOURCE: Dean, 1989.

the beach to attempt to reestablish equilibrium. If sand removed from the channel is deposited offshore rather than back into the sand-sharing system, erosion can be the only result.

Wholesale losses of beach sand have been caused by the indiscriminate dumping of inlet-dredged material offshore. Figure 2-5 estimates the amount of beach-quality sand dredged and deposited offshore from Florida's east coast inlets. This 56 million cubic yards would be sufficient to advance the sandy beach about 25 feet seaward along the entire 375-mile east coast of Florida.

Sand Mining

The loss of sand from beaches because of mining for construction and other purposes can be considerable. The effects of sand mining are similar to the effects caused when dredge material is deposited offshore.

California illustrates the scale and impacts of sand and gravel mining. For example, about 145 million tons of sand was mined in California in 1972; about 2 percent of this material was derived from beaches and dunes (Magoon et al., 1972). It is further estimated that about 9 million tons has been taken from the south end of Monterey Bay alone since the inception of the industry; about 500,000 cubic yards per year is taken from this area (Oradiwe, 1986). In many other regions sand is mined from riverbeds, and this material might otherwise be transported to beaches during periods of flooding. This mining also can produce a sand deficit, accelerating beach erosion along the coast.

Human-Induced Subsidence

Human-induced subsidence can be caused by extraction of hydrocarbons; water extraction for industrial, agricultural, and maricultural use; and loading by earth overburden. An example of extreme subsidence caused by hydrocarbon extraction is found in the Terminal Island-Long Beach region in California (National Research Council, 1987a) where the ground surface above the center of oil production subsided about 9 meters (29.5 feet) over 27 years. The subsidence was finally arrested through the use of water injection, and some rebound occurred, which in conjunction with pump pressures lifted the surface as much as 33.5 cm (1.1 feet) over an 8-year interval.

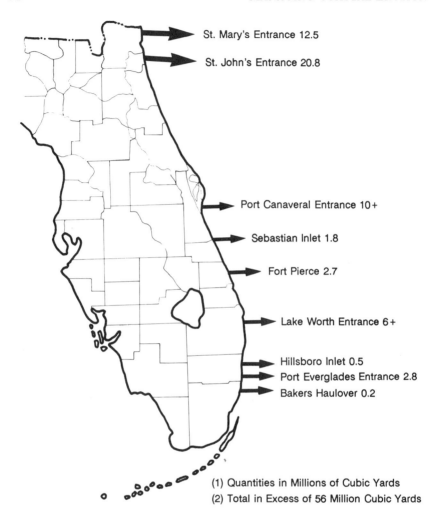

FIGURE 2-5 Estimated quantities of maintenance dredging disposed of in the deep water off the east coast of Florida. SOURCE: Dean, 1989.

Coastal land subsidence is a worldwide problem. Combined water and hydrocarbon extraction has been responsible for subsidence in the Po River Delta, Italy (Carbognin et al., 1984), and in the Galveston Bay-Houston, Texas, area. As much as 5 feet of subsidence occurred in the Galveston region between 1943 and 1964 (Gabrysch, 1969). The south end of San Francisco Bay subsided about 3 feet between 1934 and 1967; subsidence a few miles south of the bay was as much as 8 feet during the same interval, which was caused by ground water withdrawal for agricultural use (Seltz-Petrash, 1980).

Dams

Rivers are a major source of sand for U.S. Pacific coast beaches. The rate at which sand is transported to the coast increases rapidly with increased river flows; therefore, infrequent large floods are responsible for supplying most of the sand to the coast. During floods, rivers deposit sand in a river mouth delta, and waves and currents act on this episodic source, gradually transporting the sand along the coast.

The building of dams for flood and debris control, water supply, and hydroelectric power reduces the supply of sand available to the coast. By preventing floods, dam operations substantially decrease the supply of sand to beaches (National Research Council, 1987b). The Santa Clara River in southern California illustrates the effects of dams on sediment transport downstream. The average annual transport of sand and gravel from 1928 to 1975 was estimated to be 0.96 million tons (about 600,000 cubic meters). During the years when dams operated (1956 to 1975), the estimated average annual deficit of beach material was 270,000 tons (170,000 cubic meters), about a 28 percent decrease (Brownlie and Taylor, 1981). Thus, water resource planners and national decision makers should consider carefully the effects of dams on the supply of sand to beaches. Increased research and development of economical means to transport sand to beaches and alternative operations of dams would provide the information needed to make future decisions wisely.

Groins, Seawalls, and Breakwaters

An array of coastal engineering structures have been used with varying degrees of success to stabilize beaches and control erosion around U.S. coasts. Their design and utility are discussed in Chapter 3; the problem, however, is that many of these rigid structures may induce downdrift beach erosion. Because no new sand is created, their purpose is to redistribute sand along and across the beach profile or to prevent further erosion of the coast. The use of properly engineered structures has proven to be useful where properly designed, constructed, and maintained; however, their effects on adjacent shores must be carefully evaluated.

U.S. COASTLINE CHARACTERISTICS

The U.S. continental coast is highly variable in character because of differences in the geology and coastal processes. The Pacific coast (including Hawaii and Alaska) is tectonically active and is subject to earthquakes, volcanic eruptions, and tsunamis in contrast to the Atlantic and Gulf of Mexico coastal plains and the Great Lakes. The continental shelf is narrow and in places essentially nonexistent, which results in minimal attenuation of deep-water wave energy. Also, the continual passage of low-pressure cells, centered along the northern Pacific Ocean, generates large oceanic swells. The resulting wave energy is significantly higher on average than for the Atlantic and Gulf of Mexico coastlines.

Atlantic Coast

The Atlantic coast is composed of two parts: the glacial northeast coast and the southern coastal plain extending from New Jersey to Florida. Barrier islands are the dominant coastal land forms in the southern portion.

The glaciated coast extends from Maine to northern New Jersey. Scattered small pocket beaches can be found at shoreline reentrants along the erosion-resistant crystalline rock of northern New England. In contrast, the cliffs along southern New England and New York are erodible glacial deposits, with some notable exceptions such as the rocky headlands at Point Judith, Rhode Island, and Cape Anne, Massachusetts. These glacial sediments have been shaped by waves and currents into sandy barriers across embayments. Therefore, the New England coast is highly irregular, the outer shoreline becoming more smoothed by headland erosion and barrier beach accretion. For instance, the relatively small state of Massachusetts has over 1500 miles of open-coast shoreline due to its complex coastal configuration. This results in a wide range of beach types and susceptibility to storm waves and surges. In fact, Massachusetts has the largest number of recreational beaches in New England, but those along the Rhode Island coast are more urbanized and have suffered severe damage during hurricanes.

The mid-Atlantic coast, which extends from New York to Virginia, is the most urbanized shore in the country except for parts of Florida and southern California. The recreational beaches in New

York and northern New Jersey serve as playgrounds for the 15 million people in the greater New York metropolitan area. The New York to Washington metropolitan corridor exerts heavy demands for coastal recreational opportunities. As a result, land prices have soared, and there has been a coastal building boom for the last three decades. Beach erosion is a chronic problem, perhaps averaging 2 to 3 feet of recession per year along these sandy beaches. Numerous shoreline engineering projects have been attempted, particularly in northern New Jersey, to stop the shore recession. Now, however, planners are shifting emphasis away from rigid structures (e.g., seawalls, groins, etc.), and relying more on "soft" techniques such as beach nourishment.

The U.S. southeastern coast (i.e., from North Carolina to Florida) is the least urbanized along the Atlantic Coast, but this area has significant growth potential because of the availability of beachfront property. The Outer Banks of North Carolina are a long chain of barrier islands with development spread out along the shoreline. Although an increasing number of multistory condominiums are being built, the traditional building is a wooden single-family house that can be readily moved. Therefore, in this area retreating from the shore often is more attractive than beach stabilization. This alternative is plausible to a lesser extent in South Carolina and Georgia, but many islands already are too urbanized for this approach (e.g., Hilton Head, South Carolina). Also, the barrier islands in the Georgia bight (southern South Carolina to northern Florida) are generally higher in elevation, much wider, and more stable than the microtidal barriers found elsewhere along the U.S. Atlantic coast (Leatherman, 1989).

Florida should be considered separately from the other southeastern states. Its long coastline is perhaps the most important in the United States as it serves as a national and even international resort area. Recreational beaches are a major source of revenue for Florida, and state officials are considering spending tens of millions of dollars each year for beach nourishment. The Miami Beach project, completed in 1980 at a cost of $65 million for 10 miles of beach, represents the scale and magnitude of potential future projects along this rapidly urbanizing coast, which is becoming dominated by high-density, high-rise-type developments. The southern two counties, Dade and Broward, have nourished over 68 percent of their total (45 mile) shoreline.

Gulf Coast

The Gulf Coast is the lowest lying area in the United States and consequently is the most susceptible to flooding. One of the earliest extensive beach nourishment projects undertaken in the United States was in Harrison County, Mississippi, in the 1950s. The beaches have narrowed substantially since this time, and renourishment was required after Hurricane Camille in 1969 and again after Hurricanes Elena and Kate in 1985.

Louisiana has the most complex coastline in the region and also holds the distinction of having the most rapid rate of coastal erosion in the nation. This is largely a result of regional subsidence. The state of Louisiana has only two recreational beaches: Grand Isle and Holly Beach. Although Grand Isle recently was nourished, it is unlikely that the economics (i.e., the relative high cost of sand fill versus the value of property to be protected) will make such future projects feasible.

Texas has the most extensive sandy coastline in the Gulf, but much of the area is not inhabited nor easily accessible. Clearly, the city of Galveston will be maintained; the nearly century-old seawall and landfill generally have been effective in protecting this urbanized area. Elsewhere, retreat from the eroding beaches probably is the most viable alternative because land on the barrier islands is usually available for relocation.

Pacific Coast

The Pacific coast can be divided into two sections: southern California and the rest. Southern California, which extends roughly from Santa Barbara to San Diego, may be the most modified coastline in the country (although some could argue the same is true of northern New Jersey). This semiarid area has been transformed into one of the largest population centers in the United States, and explosive growth still is occurring. Because of extensive and widespread nourishment projects, many beaches reportedly are wider today than they were a century ago. The long-term trend of shore recession has been reversed successfully through coastal engineering projects (largely beach nourishment), primarily as a by-product of harbor construction. Considering the value of this real estate, the potential for continued growth, and the history of coastal projects, these public recreational beaches undoubtedly will be maintained in the future (Herron, 1980).

The northern California, Oregon, and Washington coasts can be divided into regions exposed directly to the waves and currents of the Pacific Ocean and those within tidal estuaries (e.g., San Francisco Bay and Grays Harbor), tidal lagoons, and the Puget Sound-Strait of Georgia area. The Pacific coast is mountainous and the continental shelf is narrow (Inman and Nordstrom, 1971). The major sand beaches are associated with large rivers. There are also hundreds of miles of rocky headlands and rugged mountainous regions with small steep rivers and small narrow beaches, but barrier beaches are very limited. The beaches may consist of fine sand, coarse sand, or cobbles, and some are composed of sand with cobbles underneath. The coast of Oregon is mostly mountainous rugged shoreline, but there are some sand beaches in the south. The central coastline is characterized by narrow sand beaches, low cliffs, and marine terraces. Alternating regions of both rock coast and beaches continue to the north, where wide, flat-sloped, fine sandy beaches are associated with the Columbia River.

The coast of Washington can be divided into three geomorphic regions: southern, central, and northern. The southern region is composed of wide beaches; the sand is transported as littoral drift from the Columbia River mouth. The central region consists of long beaches backed by steep seacliffs. Some sand is derived from the Columbia River mouth, but most is supplied by five other rivers that discharge into this region. The northern region is rugged, with high seacliffs and small pocket beaches of pebbles and cobbles.

Earthquake faults play an important role in the coastal geology of the Pacific coast. For example, the San Andreas Fault crosses the coastline just south of San Francisco and then crosses the coastline again and forms Bolinas Lagoon. The fault continues northwest, forms Tomales Bay, and then moves out to sea and back across land, forming Bodega Bay. The region is tectonically active, which affects the relative change in mean sea level. Also, earthquakes can be a major factor in cliff erosion as is evident from the reconnaissance survey by members of the U.S. Geological Survey, made a few days after the October 17, 1989, earthquake (Richter Scale 7.1) centered in the Santa Cruz mountains (Flinn, 1989).

The U.S. Pacific coast can be divided into a series of littoral cells, such as the Santa Monica and San Pedro cells. Sources of sand within littoral cells can be quite complex. Local rivers and coastal bluff erosion are obvious sources, together with some biogenic material. There are two major types of sinks of beach sand along the

Pacific coast: submarine canyons, such as the Monterey Canyon and the Scripps Canyon (Shepard and Wanless, 1971), and sand dunes (Cooper, 1967).

Natural events sometimes occur that have a major impact on the sources of sand in a littoral cell; for example, the Los Angeles River flowed through Ballona Gap until 1825, when it was diverted to the south during a severe flood, joining the San Gabriel River discharging into San Pedro Bay. During severe floods in 1862 and 1884, some of the Los Angeles River waters again flowed to the sea via Ballona Creek, but since then it has discharged only into San Pedro Bay (Kenyon, 1951). Historical changes in this river course also changed the location of sand discharge from the Santa Monica Cell to the San Pedro Cell.

Great Lakes

The Great Lakes coasts are composed of a wide variety of shore types, ranging from high rock bluffs to low plains and wetlands. The general character of the coasts is related directly to erosional and depositional influences of the last period of glaciation. Stream mouths and shore lakes are a distinctive feature of the coastal corridor bordering the Great Lakes. Stream mouths generally are associated with low gradient streams and in many cases form freshwater estuaries. Some shore lakes are drowned river mouths formed by the great melt of the last Ice Age; others are erosional and/or depositional features from the same period. River mouths and shore lakes contribute little sediment to the Great Lakes littoral system. Most sediment comprising Great Lakes beaches and transported in the littoral system comes directly from erosion of coastal bluffs and dunes.

A detailed inventory of shore types that compose the U.S. Great Lakes has been prepared (Great Lakes Basin Commission Framework Study, 1975). Classification of shore types was based on shore height, slope, composition, and erodibility. Shores were simply divided into nonerodible (e.g., rock bluffs) and erodible (e.g., glacial deposits and sand dunes) categories. Rates of bluff and dune erosion along Great Lakes shores vary from near zero to tens of feet per year because of annual changes in wave climate and lake level.

The U.S. coastline of Lake Superior has approximately 400 miles of nonerodible shore with areas of steep rock cliffs such as Pictured Rocks National Lakeshore. The remaining 487 miles of Lake Superior shore is erodible and varies from low-lying clay and gravel bluffs to sandy bluff-backed beaches.

Lake Michigan's 1,362 miles of shorelands has every shore type characteristic of the Great Lakes. Most impressive is the expanse of sand dunes that extend almost continuously from the Indiana Dunes National Lakeshore on southern Lake Michigan northward along Michigan's western shore to the Leelanau Peninsula. Large areas of high erodible bluffs exist along both the Michigan and Wisconsin shores, which all too often are used as prime building sites because of their exceptional natural view. By contrast, Lake Huron's 565 miles of coastline is characterized by rocky and boulder areas with some high cliff-backed beaches; elsewhere, the shore is sandy with low dunes and bluffs.

Lake Erie with 342 miles of coastline is predominately high and low erodible bluff. The southwestern area contains wetlands and a low erodible plain. This shore type changes to a low bluff and sparse dune area in western Ohio, before becoming a high erodible bluff in central and eastern Ohio. Approximately 12 percent of Lake Erie's shore is artificial fill.

Lake Ontario's 290 miles of coastline consists of bluffs of glacial material and rock outcrops at the shore. A bluff shore type fronted with narrow gravel beaches predominates along the southern shore of Lake Ontario. Bluff heights range from 20 to 60 feet and are occasionally broken by low marshes. A short reach of low dunes and barrier beaches separates this erodible bluff type shore from the erosion-resistant rock outcrops extending northward to the St. Lawrence River.

SUMMARY

The U.S. coastline exhibits a great diversity of shore types, and these variations must be considered when establishing an erosion management program. Differences in the level of development, use, and engineering structures at the shore complicate this natural diversity. Sediment sources and sinks, which are highly susceptible to human activities at the shore and in adjoining rivers and waterways, are also a major concern for erosion zone management. As a result of these multiple factors, it is necessary to consider both local conditions and broad regional issues when establishing a coastal erosion zone management program.

REFERENCES

Brownlie, W. R., and B. D. Taylor. 1981. Coastal Sediment Delivery by Major
    Rivers in Southern California. Sediment Management for Southern Califor-
    nia Mountains, Coastal Plains and Shoreline, Part C, California Institute
    of Technology, Environmental Quality Laboratory, EQL Report No. 17-C.

Carbognin, L., P. Gatto, and F. Marabini. 1984. Guidebook of the Eastern
    Po Plain (Italy): A Shore Illustration About Environmental and Land
    Subsidence. Published for use at the Third International Symposium on
    Land Subsidence, Venice, Italy, March 19-25, 1984. Printed by Ufficio
    Stampa, Comunicazione e Informazione, Comune di Madera.

Cooper, W. S. 1967. Coastal Dunes of California. Geological Society of America,
    Memoir No. 104.

Dean, R. G. 1989. Sediment interaction at modified coastal inlets: Processes
    and policies. Pp. 412-439 in Hydrodynamics and Sediment Dynamics of
    Tidal Inlets, Lecture Notes on Coastal Estuarine Studies, 29, D. Aubrey
    and L. Weishar, eds. Berlin: Springer-Verlag.

Dean, R. G., and M. Perlin. 1977. Coastal Engineering Study of Ocean City,
    Maryland. Pp. 520-542 in Proceedings of ASCE Specialty Conference on
    Coastal Sediments '77.

Dolan, T. J., P. G. Castens, C. J. Sonu, and A. K. Egense. 1987. Review of
    sediment budget methodology: Oceanside littoral cell, California. Coastal
    Sediments '87, ASCE, Vol. II, pp. 1289-1304.

Edil, T. B. 1982. Causes and Mechanics of Coastal Bluff Recession in the Great
    Lakes. Proceedings of Workshop on Bluff Slumping, Michigan Sea Grant
    Report 901, pp. 1-48.

Flinn, J. October 26, 1989. Beaches Imperiled by Weak Cliffs. San Francisco
    Examiner, pp. A1 and A9.

Gabrysch, R. K. 1969. Land-Surface Subsidence in the Houston-Galveston
    Region, Texas. Land Subsidence: Proceedings of the Tokyo Symposium,
    September 1969, Paris: UNESCO, Vol. 1, pp. 43-54.

Great Lakes Basin Commission Framework Study. 1975. Shore Use and Erosion,
    Appendix 12.

Herron, W. J. 1980. Artificial beaches in Southern California. Shore Beach
    48:3-12.

Inman, D. L., and C. E. Nordstrom. 1971. On the tectonic and morphologic
    classification of coasts. J. Geol. 79:1-21.

Johnson, J. W. 1971. The significance of seasonal beach changes in tidal
    boundaries. Shore Beach 39:26-31.

Kenyon, E. C., Jr. 1951. History of Ocean Outlets, Los Angeles Flood Control
    District. Proceedings of First Conference on Coastal Engineering, Long
    Beach, California, October 1950. Edited by J. W. Johnson, Council on
    Wave Research, The Engineering Foundation, pp. 277-282.

Leatherman, S. P. 1984. Shoreline evolution of North Assateague Island, Mary-
    land. Shore Beach 52:3-10.

Leatherman, S. P. 1985. Geomorphic and stratigraphic analysis of fire island,
    New York. Marine Geol. 63:173-195.

Leatherman, S. P. 1986. Cliff stability along western Chesapeake Bay, Maryland.
    Marine Tech. Soc. J. 20:28-36.

Leatherman, S. P. 1987. Reworking of glacial sediments along outer Cape Code: Development of Provincetown spit. Pp. 307-325 in Treatise of Glaciated Coasts, D. M. Fitzgerald and P. S. Rosen, eds. New York: Academic Press.

Leatherman, S. P. 1989 (in press). Coasts and beaches. In Heritage of Engineering Geology: The First Hundred Years. Geological Society of America.

Magoon, O. T., J. C. Haugen, and R. L. Sloan. 1972. Coastal Sand Mining in Northern California, U.S.A. Proceedings of the Thirteenth Coastal Engineering Conference, July 10-14, 1972, Vancouver, Canada, ASCE, Chapter 87, pp. 1571-1597.

National Research Council. 1987a. Responding to Changes in Sea Level: Engineering Implications. Washington, D.C.: National Academy Press.

National Research Council. 1987b. River and Dam Management: A Review of the Bureau of Reclamation's Glen Canyon Environmental Studies. Washington, D.C.: National Academy Press.

Olsen, E. J. 1977. A Study of the Effects of Inlet Stabilization at St. Mary's Entrance, Florida. Pp. 311-329 in Proceedings of ASCE Specialty Conference on Coastal Sediments '77.

Oradiwe, E. N. 1986. Sediment Budget for Monterey Bay. M.S. thesis. U.S. Naval Postgraduate School, Monterey, California.

Ritter, J. R. 1969. Preliminary Studies of Sedimentation and Hydrology in Bolinas Lagoon, Marin County, California, May 1967-June 1968. U.S. Geological Survey Open-File Report.

Seltz-Petrash, A. 1980. Subsidence—a geological problem with a political solution. Civil Eng. 52:60-63.

Shepard, F. P., and H. R. Wanless. 1971. Our Changing Coastlines. New York: McGraw-Hill.

Smith, O. P., J. M. Smith, M. A. Cialone, J. Pope, and T. L. Walton. 1985. Engineering Analysis of Beach Erosion at Homer Spit, Alaska. U.S. Army Corps of Engineers, Coastal Engineering Research Center, Misc. Paper CERC-85-13.

U.S. Army Corps of Engineers. 1967. Beach Erosion Control Study on Brevard County, Florida. Jacksonville, Fla.

Williams, S. J., and E. P. Meisburger. 1987. Sand Sources for the Transgressive Barrier Coast of Long Island, N.Y.: Evidence for Landward Transport of Shelf Sediments. Proceedings, ASCE Specialty Conference on Coastal Sediments '87, New Orleans, Louisiana.

3
Management and Approaches

INTRODUCTION

Any attempt to formulate national policies to address coastal erosion hazards confronts a task of substantial complexity. This chapter reviews some of the elements that contribute to this complexity:

- types of diversity (e.g., physical, settlement morphology, and political);
- types of private and public participants in coastal management;
- methods available for erosion hazard reduction (engineered projects) and building and land use management; and
- institutional variation of federal approaches to coastal management.

TYPES OF DIVERSITY

Federal resource management programs inevitably confront the dilemma of how to reconcile the need for uniform national policy objectives with regional diversity of geographic conditions. This issue arises, for instance, with respect to air and water quality standards, ocean dumping and disposal of dredged spoils, wetland regulations, and floodplain management. The nation's coastlines are diverse in several respects: physical, settlement, and political. Each of these classes of diversity is reviewed briefly below.

Physical Diversity

Coastal shorelines differ markedly in physical characteristics and in vulnerability to erosion, as discussed in Chapter 2. Principal types of shorelines and examples of their locations include:

- crystalline bedrock (e.g., central and northern Maine);
- eroding bluff (e.g., outer Cape Cod, Great Lakes);
- pocket beach (e.g., southern New England, California, Oregon);
- strandplain beach (e.g., Myrtle Beach, South Carolina, and Holly Beach, Louisiana);
- barrier beach (e.g., New York and Texas);
- coral reef and mangrove (e.g., South Florida); and
- coastal wetland (e.g., Louisiana).

Erosion hazards can affect each of the above except for bedrock shorelines. Erosion, as compared to accretion or stability, and its rate over time at a given point along the shoreline depend on factors such as (1) direction of littoral drift, (2) inlet dynamics, (3) sand supply, (4) short- and long-term climate fluctuations, (5) gradient of submerged ocean or lake bottom, (6) relative mean sea level, and (7) human actions affecting shoreline processes (see Table 2-1).

Settlement Diversity

Shorelines differ dramatically in their human settlement characteristics. Extensive areas of the nation's coastlines essentially are undisturbed, and much of the shore remains in a relatively undisturbed condition (e.g., national seashores, national forests, parks, wildlife refuges, military bases and recreation areas, state and local parks, and nature preserves owned by the Nature Conservancy and comparable organizations). Shorelines within such facilities generally are uninhabited except for private inholdings, which are common in several of the major national seashores (e.g., Cape Cod, Massachusetts; Fire Island, New York; Assateague Island, Virginia and Maryland; and Cape Hatteras, North Carolina) and national lakeshores (Indiana Dunes and Sleeping Bear Dunes). Substantial areas of shoreline remain in private hands but undisturbed because of lack of access, distance to population centers, physical unsuitability for development, or personal preference of the owner.

At the other extreme, shorelines may be developed extensively with port facilities or lined with commercial, industrial, or high-density residential and resort buildings. Such urbanized shorelines often are hardened by protective riprap, seawalls, or other engineered structures, which may substantially reduce or eliminate the threat of erosion to the protected area.

Efforts to protect certain segments of shoreline, however, can in some circumstances induce increased erosion on nearby unprotected shorelines. For instance, groins or jetties can deprive downdrift areas of natural sand supply. On the other hand, groin fields filled by beach nourishment have been successful.

Between the two extremes of undeveloped and highly urbanized shorelines, coastal settlement types vary widely. In the past, settlements on the shorelines were categorized into four types: (1) village, (2) urban, (3) summer, and (4) empty places (Burton et al., 1968). Today, these classifications are blurred as former summer colonies become winterized for year-round use, high-rise condominiums replace the "village" atmosphere of former small communities like Ocean City, Maryland, and major development corporations reshape the coastal landscape as at Hilton Head, South Carolina, or Amelia Island, Florida (Platt et al., 1987).

During the 1970s and 1980s, many former low-density resort communities experienced rapid structural and demographic growth. This growth was accompanied by the development of infrastructure in the form of sewer lines, water lines, access routes, and beach protection and nourishment projects, largely subsidized by the federal government. Furthermore, the availability of federal flood insurance has been identified as at least a marginal incentive to further coastal development (U.S. General Accounting Office, 1982).

Political Diversity

The nation's shorelines also show a diversity in the nature and form of political jurisdictions. Nonfederal units of public and quasi-public authority operating in coastal areas include private homeowners' associations, incorporated municipalities, special districts, counties, and states. Of course, all U.S. shorelines are subject to state jurisdiction, but the nature of that role differs considerably from one state to another. Furthermore, most regions of the nation differ in terms of substate political authority. The coast of New England, for instance, is occupied entirely by incorporated towns and cities. The minor civil divisions of New York State include incorporated villages, towns, cities, and counties. New Jersey has all of those as well as boroughs. Local government functions in Maryland and Virginia are largely provided at the county level, except for self-governing cities such as Baltimore and Virginia Beach. Elsewhere, privately owned shorelines may be subject to municipal or county jurisdiction, depending on whether or not the location in question is within an incorporated municipal unit. Furthermore, in the case of coastal barriers, local political units may be self-governing (i.e., limited to the barrier itself) or appendant (i.e., part of a larger mainland jurisdiction).

The efficacy of coastal management is related in part to the political geography of minor civil divisions of particular shorelines. Many local units tend to ignore external effects on their neighbors in their choice of approach to the management of coastal erosion (Platt et al., 1987).

These three kinds of diversity—physical, settlement, and political—serve to complicate the shaping of national policy on coastal erosion management. They suggest that no single approach is appropriate or inappropriate everywhere. Public planners and decision makers should avoid basing policies on stereotypes or preconceptions as to "typical" shorelines and their state of development and governance.

There is precedent for the administration of a national policy that is geographically selective. For example, the Coastal Barrier Resources Act (CBRA) of 1982 (discussed later in this chapter) prohibits further federal flood insurance coverage and other federal incentives to development for undeveloped and unprotected coastal barriers. This act is selective in its coverage, according to the physical character of the shoreline (coastal barrier), settlement type (undeveloped), and legal status (nonpublic and protected). The CBRA thus is one way to conduct selective implementation of federal policies designed to mitigate future losses caused by coastal erosion.

PRIVATE AND PUBLIC PARTICIPANTS IN COASTAL MANAGEMENT

The use of coastal land involves diverse private and public decision makers and other participants. The exact mix of parties and their respective roles and influence over the development of coastal property vary from one location to another. The types of diversity discussed in the preceding section—physical, settlement, and political—are major factors in determining the interested parties for any given location and development situation. Management of coastal erosion and flood hazards must recognize the variation in the interests and the varied roles of relevant parties.

Private Sector

Among private sector parties involved in coastal land development and use are

- coastal property owners,
- developers and builders,
- homeowner associations,
- neighbors or other residents affected by the use of a particular site,
- lenders, and
- realtors.

Private property owners are vested with substantial but not exclusive authority to determine the use of their land. Riparian rights traditionally entitle the waterfront land owner to embark upon the water; but the state, sometimes in conflict with those rights, is custodian of a public trust to control the use of the water and the land under it for the benefit of all. Property owners are typically the initiators of land use change (e.g., from an open to a developed condition or from one development form to another). Private owners are constrained in the exercise of this prerogative in several respects:

- Nuisance laws protect neighboring property owners and the public at large from harm caused by unreasonable use of private property, as considered in the case of *Lummis* v. *Lily*, 429 N.E.2d 1146, 1982. This case involved a stone groin on Cape Cod, Massachusetts, and lists the factors to be applied in determining if the structure was "reasonable" and therefore immune from a damage claim by a neighbor.
- Covenants and deed restrictions can arise through private terms of a subdivision instrument of conditions, through retention of certain rights by a prior seller that "run with the land" or by other means. Such private restrictions, when legal in purpose and

recorded properly, are enforceable against private owners whose land is thereby encumbered. These restrictions include

- municipal/county zoning and subdivision regulations;
- state building codes, wetland and floodplain regulations, and coastal zone management regulations; and
- federal environmental regulations.

Developers/builders may or may not hold an ownership interest in the site in question. They may operate in partnership with the owner and/or with other investors. Professional developers/builders are held to a higher level of responsibility with respect to the quality and safety of the resulting structure than nonprofessional owners. The possibility of professional liability affecting the developer/builder and professional advisors (e.g., architects, engineers, and lawyers) may be a constraint on unwise construction in erosion-prone locations.

Homeowner associations are private nonprofit corporations established by a developer to own and manage the common facilities of a particular residential subdivision. An association also can serve as "watchdog" to enforce subdivision deed restrictions. The membership of the association consists of the owners of all lots in the subdivision. In coastal areas homeowner associations may own and manage beach and shoreline property on behalf of the subdivision lot owners.

Neighbors and other residents have a voice in the local zoning process through mandatory public notice and hearing provisions of state law.

Lenders include banks, savings and loan associations, pension funds, insurance companies, and other institutions that finance land development. Lenders that are "federally related" (e.g., insured or regulated by federal agencies) are required to ascertain and inform borrowers as to whether a site is located within a "special flood hazard area" identified by the National Flood Insurance Program (NFIP). If so, the borrower is required to purchase flood insurance for the acquisition or improvement of structures on such a site (42 USC Section 4104a). This requirement could be extended to erosion-prone areas not now included in flood hazard zones.

Realtors have a professional duty to disclose flood or erosion hazards known to them or ascertainable from published maps of the NFIP. Like developers, realtors can be held liable to a buyer for concealing or failing to ascertain the existence of such hazards.

Public Sector

Public participants in coastal land development and management include

- incorporated municipalities (e.g., villages, boroughs, towns, cities);
- counties;
- special districts;
- states; and the
- federal government.

The roles performed by various tiers and units of government differ from one state and location to another, as discussed in the preceding section. Briefly, the principal roles of public entities that relate to development in erosion-prone coastal areas are the following:

- land ownership (e.g., national, state, local parks);
- police power (e.g., zoning, subdivision, environmental, and hazard mitigation regulations);
- infrastructure funding and/or operation (e.g., roads, bridges, causeways, sewer and water lines); and
- development (e.g., convention centers, cultural facilities, sports complexes).

Not all of these roles pertain to each tier of public authority. The following matrix suggests, in general terms, the functions of respective types of governmental units, although these vary among states and localities (Table 3-1). This matrix suggests that the role common to all levels of government is the funding and/or operation of the physical infrastructure. This function typically requires multilevel participation in the form of funding, design, licensing, operation, and inspection of facilities.

A national program for coastal erosion management must address the siting and design of public infrastructure that encourages development in erosion hazard areas. (Eroding shores within designated units of the Coastal Barrier Resource System already are off limits to federal infrastructure funding and flood insurance under the CBRA of 1982.)

In summary, the development and management of land subject to coastal erosion are influenced by the actions of diverse private and public participants. A national policy on coastal erosion must acknowledge this complexity and seek to achieve erosion/flood loss reduction through multiple approaches involving different classes of

TABLE 3-1 Functions of Governmental Units

	Coastal Landowner	Police Power	Infrastructure Provider/ Funding	Developer	Land Use Planning
Municipality	x	x	x	x	x
Special district	o		x	x	—
County	o	x*	x*	x	o
State	x	x	x	—	x
Federal	x	x	x	—	o

NOTE: x, major role in most states; o, minor role in most states; and —, not a role in most states.

*Primarily for unincorporated areas.

participants and actions (e.g., local planning and zoning, public land acquisition, withholding of infrastructure funding, and clarification of professional duties of lenders, developers, and realtors). All approaches require improved public understanding of the nature and implications of coastal erosion.

RELEVANT FEDERAL PROGRAMS

Since the 1930s, Congress has created a variety of programs and initiatives relating to management of coastal areas, including the Great Lakes. These have pursued a number of objectives, some of them in conflict with others (e.g., navigation, national defense, public recreation, riparian rights, public trust for underwater lands, protection of fish and wildlife resources, economic development, mitigation of pollution, and reduction of losses owing to natural hazards, including coastal erosion). Federal constitutional powers involved in these efforts have included spending power, taxation power, interstate commerce power, and regulatory police power. Approaches taken have varied widely from one program to another. Those of primary importance to this discussion are the following:

1. U.S. Army Corps of Engineers: coastal protection works, navigation improvements, and regulation of dredge and fill.

2. U.S. Department of the Interior: acquisition of national parks and national wildlife refuges.

3. U.S. Environmental Protection Agency: regulation of ocean dumping, discharges into waters of the United States, research on sea level rise, etc.

4. National Oceanic and Atmospheric Administration/Office of Ocean and Coastal Resource Management: funding and technical assistance to support state coastal zone management programs.

5. Federal Emergency Management Agency/Federal Insurance Administration: mapping of coastal hazard areas and administration of the NFIP.

6. Coastal Barriers Resources Act of 1982.

The following sections briefly review these programs, followed by a more detailed discussion of the coastal aspects of the NFIP.

U.S. Army Corps of Engineers

The Army Corps of Engineers (COE) has been engaged in navigation improvements of the nation's waterways, both intracoastal and inland, since 1824. The Intracoastal Waterway extending from Texas to New Jersey began prior to World War II and has contributed to the public enjoyment and economic development along the Atlantic and Gulf coastlines. COE river and harbor projects, such as channel dredging and inlet stabilization, have similarly promoted economic and recreational usage of estuarine areas, bays, and harbors along the nation's ocean and Great Lakes shorelines.

COE coastal erosion activities have included the construction of seawalls, jetties, and groin fields and beach restoration and nourishment projects. These projects have been approved by Congress with varying cost-sharing ratios. The nonfederal percentage of total project costs varies depending on local interest; however, many project costs are shared on a 50/50 basis. Since 1970 the National Environmental Policy Act has required that an Environmental Impact Statement be prepared for COE coastal protection and navigation projects, which are deemed to be "major federal actions significantly affecting the human environment."

In addition to its civil works functions, the COE administers several permit programs regulating the discharge of material into navigable waters and all construction therein. Of particular relevance to the management of coastal areas subject to erosion and sea level rise, COE administers (except in Michigan where the state has assumed 404 administrative authority) the "dredge and fill" permit program under Section 404 of the Federal Clean Water Act. Pursuant to guidelines established by the U.S. Environmental Protection Agency (EPA), COE must approve any proposed construction including dredge or fill in "waters of the United States," including wetlands bordering navigable waters (Platt, 1987). In cooperation with EPA, COE thus plays a critical role in relicensing of large- or small-scale development in coastal and estuarine wetlands. This encompasses much of the ongoing development in areas subject to coastal floods and erosion.

U.S. Department of the Interior

The National Park Service (NPS) and the Fish and Wildlife Service (FWS) of the Department of the Interior (DOI) own and manage substantial land holdings along the nation's eroding coastlines. Each agency controls extensive areas of open coast shorelines, coastal barriers, estuarine wetlands, zones of fish migration, and eroding shorelines on the Great Lakes.

Most NPS areas subject to coastal erosion are located within the nation's 10 national seashores and four national lakeshores. These were established during the 1960s and 1970s, beginning with the authorization of the Cape Cod National Seashore in 1961 (Cape Hatteras was designated a national park in 1937). Coastal erosion has adversely affected many of these facilities, notably Cape Cod, where a single winter storm in 1978 destroyed parking lots, access roads, visitor facilities, and a national landmark, the "Outermost House." The Cape Hatteras Lighthouse is another major national historic landmark managed by the NPS that is threatened by coastal erosion. An NRC study of options to preserve that lighthouse recommended that it be moved landward rather than constructing shore protection structures (National Research Council, 1988). Another NPS area threatened by severe coastal erosion is Indiana Dunes National Lakeshore. Jetties built during the 1970s have interfered with sediment transport and caused the loss of most of the area's once impressive sand beach. (In 1989, some beach has reappeared with lower lake levels.)

FWS administers the National Wildlife Refuge System, along with several dozen units in coastal areas. In some cases, such as Assateague Island (Maryland and Virginia), FWS manages a wildlife refuge directly adjacent to an NPS facility. Wildlife refuges by definition have few human-made artifacts to be threatened by coastal erosion. Nevertheless, the gradual submergence of existing wetland habitat is an important long-term issue for the FWS.

U.S. Environmental Protection Agency

The EPA promulgates guidelines for the administration of the Section 404 Dredge and Fill Program for coastal and inland wetlands. An important provision of these guidelines is that non-water-dependent uses are disfavored in wetlands. The COE cannot issue a Section 404 dredge and fill permit for such an activity if an appropriate upland site is available. The burden of proof lies with the applicant to demonstrate that such a site is not available.

To obtain permits in 404-protected areas, the applicant must provide "mitigation" of adverse impacts through appropriate design, location, and, in some cases, restoration or creation of other wetlands. Building techniques designed to mitigate harm to wetlands also may be useful in averting threats to the same structures from storm surge and shore erosion. EPA is also conducting a series of studies of major embayments under the National Estuary Program.

National Oceanic and Atmospheric Administration

The Coastal Zone Management (CZM) Act of 1972 established a joint federal-state process for coastal zone planning and management. The federal CZM program is administered by the Office of Ocean and Coastal Resource Management (OCRM) of the National Oceanic and Atmospheric Administration (NOAA). The act declared a national policy favoring better management of coastal land and water resources, cited the need for federal-state collaboration in planning for nonfederal portions of the coastal zone, and authorized funds to assist states in developing and administering their own coastal management plans.

The federal CZM program does not set mandatory federal standards, nor does it require the issuing of federal licenses or permits by OCRM. Instead, the program facilitates state and local coastal zone planning through funding and technical assistance. To be eligible for OCRM funding, a state plan must address a number of public policy issues, such as navigation, habitat protection, economic development, public recreation and access to shorelines, scientific research, energy development, and natural hazard mitigation. As of 1989, 29 of the 35 eligible states and territories bordering oceans and the Great Lakes were approved by OCRM to receive ongoing CZM funding. This funding supports both state and local coastal planning staff and assists in acquiring and/or upgrading coastal facilities and implementing state plans.

Coastal management programs are required to include a "planning process for (a) assessing the effects of shore erosion (however caused), and (b) studying and evaluating ways to control, or lessen the impact of, such erosion, and to restore areas adversely affected by such erosion" (CZMA 305 (b) (9)). The implementation of the erosion planning process has been an eligible expenditure of coastal management funds, particularly to mitigate for erosion in local land use decisions. Coastal management funds have been used to develop legislation that requires development to be set back from the hazards of storm surge, tsunamis, and erosion. Eleven states have minimum setback requirements, most developed with CZM funds. Funding also has been used to map erosion areas and review permits.

When development is already located in hazard-prone areas, coastal zone management programs have applied other appropriate management strategies. They have developed evacuation plans, paid for the construction and restoration of sand dunes, and designed protection structures and beach restoration plans.

Federal Emergency Management Agency

The NFIP was established in 1968, and it has become the principal expression of federal policy on riverine and coastal flood hazards. The NFIP is administered by the Federal Emergency Management Agency (FEMA). The NFIP offers flood insurance coverage of structures and their contents within some 1,200 participating coastal communities. To be eligible for federal insurance, a community must adopt and enforce floodplain management regulations for new development in flood hazard areas mapped by the NFIP. As of August 31, 1987, coastal communities accounted for 1.4 million policies (71.6 percent of NFIP total) and $120 billion of insurance coverage in effect (76.9 percent of NFIP total) (U.S. General Accounting Office, 1988). An unknown but substantial amount of this coverage pertains to shoreline structures threatened by erosion. The NFIP to date has not effectively addressed erosion as a contributing factor to flood losses, and, in the case of erodible bluffs, as a hazard in its own right apart from floods. The NFIP is examined more closely in Chapter 4.

Coastal Barrier Resources Act

The CBRA prohibited certain federal incentives to development of undeveloped coastal barriers. Among the incentives expressly prohibited are flood insurance under the NFIP; coastal protection projects of the COE; and federal grants for roads, bridges, causeways, water and sewer lines, and similar facilities (Platt, 1985). The CBRA specified 167 segments of undeveloped coastal barriers along the Atlantic and Gulf coasts that are not publicly owned or otherwise protected. A proposal submitted to Congress in 1987 recommended expansion of the "Coastal Barrier Resource System" to include additional areas along the Great Lakes as well as the Atlantic and Gulf of Mexico.

METHODS FOR EROSION HAZARD REDUCTION

Introduction

Various options exist to reduce the erosion hazard to public and private buildings and infrastructure. These options include soft structural (e.g., beach nourishment) approaches, hard structural approaches (e.g., seawalls, revetments, groins, offshore breakwaters, etc.), building and land use restrictions (e.g., setback requirements), and relocation of existing structures from eroding shores. Both soft and hard structural solutions are categorized here under "shoreline engineering." It should be kept in mind that many developed coasts already are using both hard and/or soft forms of shoreline engineering.

Shoreline Engineering

BEACH NOURISHMENT

Beach nourishment involves excavation from one site and placing in another site large quantities of sand on an existing but retreating beach to advance the shoreline seaward. The material usually is placed on the beach at a slope steeper than the natural beach so there will be a period of perhaps several years during which profile equilibration will occur. In addition, the shoreline protuberance will induce additional components of longshore sediment transport away from the original location.

Dean (1989) has shown that the additional beach benefits from a beach nourishment project depend markedly on the quality of the sand placed. Figure 3-1 presents four cases in which the same amount of material of varying sand sizes results in markedly differing equilibrated beach widths. Ideally, for greatest benefit, the sand should be as coarse as or coarser than the native sand. However, knowledge about sediment transport does not include adequate information concerning the influence of grain-size distribution.

The longevity of a beach nourishment project placed on a long uninterrupted shoreline varies directly with the square of the project length of shoreline and inversely with the 2.5 power of the representative wave height (Dean, 1989; see Figure 3-1). If beach fill is placed downdrift of a littoral barrier or where the longshore sediment transport (supply) has been reduced otherwise, the loss rates will depend primarily on the supply deficit owing to the interruption. Projects so located should be considered as "feeder beaches" rather than nourishment projects.

Many examples of both successful and unsuccessful beach nourishment projects exist. Successful projects include Miami Beach, Florida, where 14 million cubic yards of sand was placed over a 10-mile beach during the period 1976 to 1981 at a cost of $64 million. The first renourishment in 1987 placed 300,000 cubic yards, which amounts to a loss rate of less than 0.3 percent per year. The Indialantic Beach in Florida is regarded as an unsuccessful beach nourishment project. Approximately 500,000 cubic yards of sand was placed along 2 miles of beach. This is considered a relatively low density (≈ 50 cubic yards per foot). Beach monitoring was conducted out to wading depth, so the true volumetric loss could not be ascertained. One year after project construction, little volume remained within the portions of the profile encompassed by the wading surveys.

In areas where material is placed near a sand sink, such as a deepened channel, terminal structures to stabilize the fill may be justified. Although knowledge of the performance of beach nourishment projects has improved over the past few decades, the capability to predict the loss rates associated with a beach nourishment project are still probably no better than about ±30 percent. A great deal of this uncertainty is due to the lack of quantification of wave and sediment conditions and the lack of ability to forecast storms.

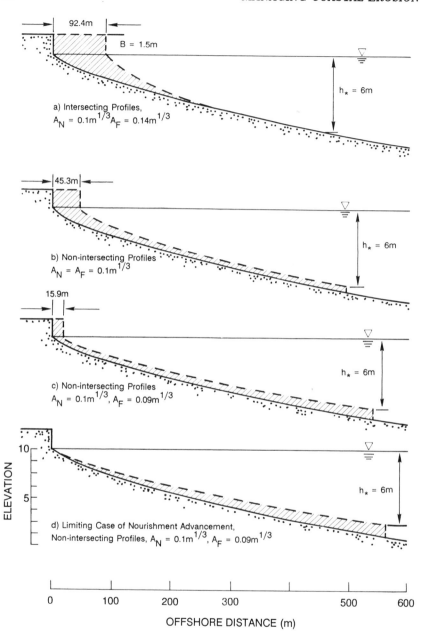

FIGURE 3-1   Effect of nourishment material scale parameter, A_F, on width of resulting dry beach. Four examples of decreasing A_F. SOURCE: Dean, 1989.

GROINS

Groins are structures built perpendicular to the shore that may be constructed of timber, concrete, metal sheet piling, or rock. They may be built singly or in a series. Groins are intended to reduce longshore sediment transport; thus, when placed on an open coast, they widen the beach on the updrift side. Groins designed with heights that match the beach profile have less potential of causing downdrift beach erosion than a high profile and/or long structure that may divert water and sediment offshore.

Groins often have been used improperly in the past, and some states have prohibited their construction. Groins used with care, however, have the potential to stabilize beach fills. A type of adjustable groin has been used in Deerfield Beach, Florida, whose upper elevation may be maintained slightly above the sand level (Deerfield encompasses 52 such groins). In this way, the structures can be adjusted to ensure that they function primarily to stabilize material in place rather than trap material in transport. A field of groins or groins placed as terminal structures might be particularly appropriate to retain material placed in a beach nourishment project. Additionally, a field of groins or a single long "terminal structure" may be suitable near the end of a littoral system such as adjacent to a channel entrance.

SEAWALLS AND REVETMENTS

Properly engineered seawalls and revetments can protect the land behind them without causing adverse effects to the fronting beaches. Seawalls normally are built on shorelines that are eroding. Often, however, the seawall is blamed for the additional erosion that occurs (O'Brien and Johnson, 1980). This happens if they are not designed and constructed properly and can cause adverse impacts on adjacent property. Additionally, seawalls and revetments are expensive and require proper maintenance.

A survey of 70 technical papers and reports on the effects of seawalls on beaches (Kraus, 1987), followed by a more extensive study with an additional 30 references, led Kraus (1988) to conclude the following:

"It is concluded that beach change near seawalls, both in magnitude and variation, is similar to that on beaches without seawalls, if a sediment supply exists. Sediment volumes eroded by storms at beaches with and without seawalls are comparable, as are poststorm recovery rates. In addition, the shape of the beach profile after construction of a seawall is similar to the preconstruction shape if a sediment supply exists, showing the same number of bars with approximately the same volumes and relative locations. The form of the erosional response to storms at seawalls is typically different. Limited evidence indicates that the subaqueous nearshore profile on a sediment-deficient coast with seawalls does not steepen indefinitely, but approaches an equilibrium configuration compatible with the coarser-grained particles comprising the bottom sediment."

As pointed out by Dean (1986), the only principle that is definitely established is the one of "sediment conservation." Coastal armoring (e.g., a riprap or seawall) neither adds to nor removes sand from the sediment system but may be responsible for the redistribution of sand and can prevent sand from entering the system. Although armoring can cause additional localized scour during storms, both in front of and at the ends of the armoring, there are no factual data to support claims that armoring causes profile steepening, increased longshore transport, transport of sand to a substantial distance offshore, or delayed poststorm recovery.

Low-profile seawalls or dikes can be used to retain a beach or fillet of sand above the normal beach profile level. Such structures are referred to as perched beaches and may exist as single-level or terraced structures.

OFFSHORE BREAKWATERS

Offshore or detached breakwaters typically are constructed from rock or concrete armor units and protect the shoreline by reducing wave energy reaching it. They also promote sediment deposition leeward of the structures. Most offshore breakwaters built for shore protection are segmented and detached; thus, they provide substantial protection to the shoreline without completely stopping longshore sand transport. They do not deflect and relocate currents, like breakwaters that project from the land. Unlike seawalls, revetments, or bulkheads, breakwaters aid in the retention of the beach because they reduce wave energy. A main disadvantage is that they are more expensive to build than land-based structures.

Segmented, detached breakwaters have been used successfully to protect shorelines from erosion in many countries such as Japan, Spain, Italy, and Israel. The use of these structures in the United States has been limited to a few sites in Massachusetts, Ohio, Pennsylvania, Virginia, and Hawaii. Submerged breakwaters, or artificial reefs, have been used in many parts of the world, notably in Italy but recently in Florida. They may be composed of sunken barges or ships or any heavy objects that break up wave action. The costs can be much less than for breakwaters that project above the water surface because they do not have to absorb the full wave impact, but merely cause storm waves to break and spill their energy in turbulence.

SAND BYPASSING

Inlets, navigation channels, and harbor entrances all interrupt the natural flow of sediment transport along the shoreline. The interrupted flow of sand is diverted either offshore in ebb tide shoals, into bays or lagoons in flood tide shoals, or in navigation channels. They generally cause shoaling and downdrift migration of channels, which require frequent dredging in order to maintain safe navigation. As a result, erosion occurs downdrift of the interrupted coastline. Sand bypassing, by either a fixed or floating pumping system, restores the natural flow of sand to the downdrift shorelines and reduces the need for channel dredging. Successful operations of this type exist in many countries such as Australia, Japan, and South Africa. In Florida the use of two fixed bypassing plants for a period of 30 years suggests the feasibility of such systems to alleviate human-induced erosion downdrift from inlet control structures. Floating dredge (temporary) bypass operations also have been used in the United States. One example is a federal project at Channel Islands Harbor, California, where over 1 million cubic yards of sand is bypassed on a biennial basis past two harbor entrances to restore eroding downdrift beaches (Herron and Harris, 1966).

DUNE BUILDING

Natural sand dunes are formed by winds blowing onshore over the beach, transporting sand landward. Grass and sometimes bushes grow on sand dunes, creating a natural barrier against sea attack. The dunes provide a reservoir of beach sand during severe storms and thus help prevent flood and wave damage to adjacent property. In areas where substantial dunes exist, the poststorm beach width can be greater than the prestorm width.

Attempts have been made to mimic nature by promoting the formation of artificial dunes. Artificial dunes have been created in many countries around the world, as well as in the United States. States where large-scale dune construction has occurred include North Carolina, Texas, Florida, and New Jersey.

PROPERTY OF
METHODIST COLLEGE LIBRARY
FAYETTEVILLE, N. C.

Building and Land Use Management

Since the advent of the NFIP in 1968, legal and institutional ("nonstructural") measures have become important mechanisms used to reduce the vulnerability of coastal and riverine structures to flood and erosion losses. Planners have often seen engineered responses to coastal erosion as unsuitable from an economic and environmental perspective, especially when used to protect privately owned, lower density residential development. One promising approach to coastal management is to influence the location, elevation, and design of new or substantially redeveloped structures through public building and land use controls.

The NFIP in particular has fostered the adoption of floodplain management standards by some 1200 coastal communities nationally, containing an estimated 43 million people (Congressional Research Service, 1987). Like their counterparts along inland floodplains, these communities must require minimum elevation of new structures above estimated 100-year flood ("base flood") levels that include the effect of wave heights. These land development restrictions generally have been held to be constitutional (Kusler, 1982).

SETBACK REQUIREMENTS

Coastal construction standards under the NFIP have emphasized elevation rather than horizontal displacement. New buildings on substantial pilings up to 20 feet above grade are a familiar site in recently built communities along the Atlantic and Gulf coasts. But horizontal displacement is required under the flood insurance program's minimum standards, only to the extent that new buildings in coastal high-hazard zones (V-zones) (see Figure 3-2) must be "located landward of the reach of mean high tide" and must not alter dunes or mangrove stands (44 CFR Section 60.3(e)). Even these minimal requirements do not apply to coastal A zones (e.g., bayside or other non-open ocean shorelines). Where either V-zone or A-zone coastal shores are experiencing erosion, further horizontal displacement of new or rebuilt structures is needed.

A number of coastal states have established horizontal setbacks for new construction at the individual state level (Hildreth, 1980; Maloney and O'Donnell, 1978). According to an unpublished NOAA memorandum (Houlahan, 1988), there are three basic approaches states have taken: (1) natural resource protection statutes, (2) fixed setback lines, and (3) average annual recession rate setbacks. The

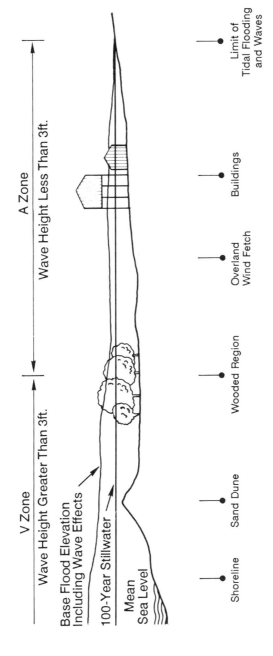

FIGURE 3-2 Illustration of FEMA's current V-zone and coastal A-zone criteria.

first category includes states such as Massachusetts and Wisconsin that place limitations upon development in wetlands or on dune systems. These requirements are not specifically designed to address erosion.

Fixed setback lines involve a minimum specified distance (e.g., 100 feet in Delaware) from a reference feature. Types of physical reference features include (1) seaward toe of primary dunes, (2) line of vegetation, (3) edge of eroding bluff, (4) mean high water, or (5) a specified elevation contour. These features may move whenever erosion occurs.

Florida established a "coastal construction control line" for each of its 24 sandy beach coastal counties based on the estimated inland reach of a 100-year storm event. Construction is not prohibited seaward of this line, but a state permit must be obtained and construction must conform to state design standards (Shows, 1978).

At least seven states use "average annual erosion rate" (AAER) setbacks to mark the minimum setback for new construction. Michigan and North Carolina impose a 30-year setback on smaller structures; North Carolina also imposes a 60-year setback on larger ones. These guidelines have been incorporated into the Upton-Jones Amendment to the NFIP. (See further discussion in Chapter 4.)

THE TAKING ISSUE

Since the late 1960s, land use and building regulations have been applied widely by states and local governments to regulate development in areas subject to special limitations such as floodplains and wetlands. Such regulations often impose severe restrictions on the rights of private landowners to fill or build in designated flood hazard or wetland areas. A variety of such measures were challenged in court during the 1960s and early 1970s under the theory of "taking issue," that is, that the measure is so restrictive that it "takes" the value of the property without compensation in violation of the Fifth Amendment to the U.S. Constitution. Despite some early setbacks (e.g., *Morris County Land Investment Co.* v. *Township of Parsipanny-Troy Hills*, 193 A. 2d 232, New Jersey [1963], most decisions have upheld the public regulations. Two landmark opinions issued in 1972 in Massachusetts (*Turnpike Realty Co.* v. *Town of Dedham*, 284 N.E. 2d 891) and Wisconsin (*Just* v. *Marinette County*,

201 N.W. 2d 761) upheld public restrictions in a riverine floodplain and a lakeshore wetland, respectively. Relatively few judicial decisions have been concerned specifically with measures intended to mitigate the effects of coastal flooding and erosion. An early California opinion (*McCarthy* v. *City of Manhatten Beach*, 264 P. 2d 932 [1954]) upheld a "beach recreation district" that prevented the owner of three-fifths of a mile of Pacific beach shoreline from building on his property. In upholding the zoning measure, the court noted that the property "is, from time to time, subject to erosion and replacement by reason of storms and wave action of the Pacific Ocean" (264 P. 2d, at 934). Prevention of construction in areas known to have been inundated in Pacific coastal storms in the 1930s was held to serve a valid public purpose. The right to charge admission to users of this private beachfront was considered adequate economic return to the owner.

A 1966 New Jersey decision (*Spiegle* v. *Borough of Beach Haven*, 218 A. 2d 129) specifically addressed public setback regulations designed to mitigate coastal flooding and erosion hazards on an Atlantic Coast barrier island. Beach Haven prohibited new construction seaward of a building line established 20 feet inland of a designated dune area. The New Jersey Supreme Court sustained this setback regulation in the strongest possible terms:

"The borough . . . adduced unrebutted proof that it would be unsafe to construct houses oceanward of the building line . . . because of the possibility that they would be destroyed during a severe storm—a result which occurred during the storm of March 1962. Additionally, defendant submitted proof that there was great peril to life and health arising through the likely destruction of streets, sewer water and gas mains, and electric power lines in the proscribed area in an ordinary storm. The gist of this testimony was that such regulation prescribed only such conduct as good husbandry would dictate that plaintiffs should impose on the use of their own lands." (218 A.2d, at 135)

Although the *Spiegle* decision technically is limited in its effect to New Jersey, it provides a rationale that could be adopted by state courts elsewhere. Surprisingly few opinions have appeared in the last two decades concerned with coastal setbacks per se (e.g., *Town of Indialantic* v. *McNulty*, 400 So. 2d 1227, Florida [1981]). In view of the widespread approval of floodplain and wetland regulations generally, there is a strong legal basis for the broader use of setbacks for coastal construction based on the best available scientific estimates of future erosion rates.

RELOCATION

Relocation of existing structures from eroding and/or flood-prone shorelines has long been a neglected mechanism for responding to shoreline retreat. The technical feasibility of moving small or medium-size structures has been established. As early as 1888, a three-story seaside hotel was moved in one piece a distance of 495 feet landward from an eroding shoreline at Coney Island, New York (*Scientific American*, 1888). In 1988, the National Research Council (NRC) Committee on Options to Preserve Cape Hatteras Lighthouse recommended that the 2,800-ton lighthouse be relocated physically in preference to in situ efforts to stabilize the retreating shoreline (National Research Council, 1988). The committee concluded that moving the lighthouse would be technically and economically feasible.

Relocation as a widespread adjustment to shore erosion is most likely to be cost effective for smaller structures, particularly one- and two-story residential buildings. Private residential development usually is not eligible for federally sponsored shoreline protection projects. Certain states, including North Carolina and Maine, discourage or prohibit further hardening of residential shorelines, although "soft" forms of stabilization such as beach nourishment may be permitted (e.g., in several Florida communities where nonfederal beach nourishment has been accomplished).

Relocation encounters a number of institutional and economic impediments. Structures on deep lots may gain sufficient protection by relocating landward on the same lot (the most common practice in Michigan). However, if sufficient space is not available on the same lot, an alternative site must be acquired and prepared. This increases the cost of relocation substantially. It also may incur problems of zoning; mortgage refinancing; and provision of sewer, water, and road access. The alternative site may lack the view and/or direct shoreline access that are often the reason for waterfront property ownership.

However, a structure threatened by imminent collapse essentially is valueless and poses substantial potential costs to the community in terms of lost tax revenue, deterioration related to disinvestment/abandonment, clearance of wreckage, casualty loss deductions from income tax liability, disaster relief payments, and flood insurance loss payments. Relocation therefore may be a desirable public goal (e.g., through Upton-Jones payments as discussed in Chapter 4). Relocation involving any public subsidy of support should involve a landward distance at least equal to established setbacks for new construction.

CONSTRUCTION REQUIREMENTS

Damage to structures located along the shore in some cases can be reduced by relatively straightforward engineering and construction procedures to ensure the building's survivability during a 100-year storm event. In particular, the following is recommended if the building is likely to be subject to damage during the event:

1. The lower horizontal structural members should be elevated above the 100-year wave crest elevation, the calculations taking into account the eroded profile.

2. Pilings on low dunes should be embedded to an adequate depth to ensure structural integrity during a 100-year storm tide and associated erosional event.

3. Connections of structural members should withstand anticipated 100-year wind loading.

Although the above would increase cost of construction in the coastal zone, the effect would be to reduce substantially the demolition claims against the program and increase the relocation activity following storms. As proposed, these recommendations would only be effective for new structures; however, the economic feasibility of retrofitting existing structures within a designated erosional zone should be investigated. To ensure construction in accordance with requirements discussed here, certification should be required by a registered engineer or architect.

OTHER COMMUNITY MANAGEMENT TOOLS

A *land acquisition* program is another strategy to cope with coastal erosion management. This is appropriate where erosion-prone areas can be acquired and preserved for recreation, open space, or other appropriate public purposes. Such programs generally include specific criteria and priorities for acquisition, identify funding sources, and set timetables for action. Potential federal funding sources include, among others, Section 1362 of the National Flood Insurance Act, the Land and Water Conservation Fund, and Section 306A of the Federal Coastal Zone Management Act. The community plans also can identify state and local resources that will be devoted to this program.

The scope and implementation of both the relocation and acquisition programs adopted should be a factor in setting flood insurance rates for the community. This would ensure that policy holders in those communities doing the most to prevent future flood and erosion losses receive the greatest benefit. This integration of the insurance and erosion management aspects of the programs through community risk assessment could be a critical aspect of producing an actuarially sound program that effectively encourages loss prevention.

Public infrastructure investment includes financing coastal erosion structures where appropriate (e.g., nourishment, seawalls, jetties, and breakwaters). It also includes the location of public infrastructure (e.g., roads, water pipes, and sewers) that influences the location and density of developments and poststorm redevelopment, roads, water, sewer, and the like and those planned to reduce future losses. Plans and standards can be adopted to assure that new public development itself is located away from erosion hazard areas where such is feasible and is designed to avoid inducing additional private development in hazard areas. Where applicable, attention also can be given to establishing a program to identify and finance appropriate shore protection investments.

Community education programs can inform land owners, developers, realtors, purchasers, and the public about flood and erosion hazards, associated public cost, and local management requirements for hazard areas. These programs can include the physical posting of signs showing flood elevations, flood boundaries, and the potential extent of erosion and the ready availability of flood hazard and erosion rate maps.

SUMMARY

This chapter has reviewed several variables that influence the management of coastal erosion areas. These include diversity of (1) physical shoreline type (as reflected in different degrees of susceptibility to erosion), (2) settlement types and patterns, and (3) political governance. Furthermore, private and public interests play various roles from one segment of shoreline to another. This chapter summarized federal coastal programs with which the NFIP must interact. The NFIP itself is a primary vehicle for implementing a national erosion policy and is the subject of the next chapter.

Finally, this chapter has reviewed methods of response to erosion hazards that include both engineered and nonengineered measures.

The former include "hard" projects, such as seawalls, jetties, groin fields, and breakwaters, as well as "soft" measures, notably beach nourishment and dune restoration. Nonengineered measures include land use and building regulations and relocation, retrofitting, or demolition of existing structures.

REFERENCES

Burton, I., R. W. Kates, and R. E. Snead. 1968. The Human Ecology of Coastal Flood Hazard in Megalopolis. Research Paper No. 115. Chicago: University of Chicago Department of Geography.

Congressional Research Service. 1987. Managing Coastal Development Through the Coastal Zone Management and Flood Insurance Programs: Experience to Date and the Views from Selected States. Report ENR 88-254. Washington, D.C.: CRS, p. 28.

Dean, R. G. 1986. Coastal Armoring: Effects, Principles and Mitigation. Twentieth Coastal Engineering Conference: Proceedings of the International Conference, November 9-14, 1986, Taipei, Taiwan, ASCE, Vol. III, Chapter 135, pp. 1843-1857.

Dean, R. G. 1989. Sediment interaction at modified coastal inlets: Processes and policies. Pp. 412-439 in Hydrodynamics and Sediment Dynamics of Tidal Inlets, Lecture Notes on Coastal Estuarine Studies, 29, D. Aubrey and L. Weishar, eds. Berlin: Springer-Verlag.

Herron, W. J., and R. L. Harris. 1966. Littoral Bypassing and Beach Restoration in the Vicinity of Port Hueneme, Calif. Proceedings, 10th Conference on Coastal Engineering, Tokyo, Japan, September 1966, ASCE, Vol. 1, pp. 651-675.

Hildreth, R. 1980. Coastal natural hazards management. Oreg. L. Rev. 59:201.

Houlahan, J. M. 1988. Analysis of state construction setbacks to manage development in coastal high hazard areas. Unpublished NOAA memorandum, April 26.

Kraus, N. C. 1987. The Effects of Seawalls on the Beach: A Literature Review. Proceedings, Coastal Sediments '87, New Orleans, Louisiana, May 12-14, 1987, ASCE.

Kraus, N. C. 1988. The Effects of Seawalls on the Beach: Extended Literature Review. J. Coastal Research, Special Issue No. 4, Autumn 1988, pp. 1-28.

Kusler, J. A. 1982. Regulation of Flood Hazard Areas to Reduce Flood Losses. Washington, D.C.: U.S. Water Resources Council.

Maloney, F. E., and A. J. O'Donnell. 1978. Drawing the line at the oceanfront: The development of the coastal zone. U. Fla. L. Rev. 30:383.

National Research Council. 1988. Saving Cape Hatteras Lighthouse from the Sea, Options and Policy Implementations. Washington, D.C.: National Academy Press.

O'Brien, M. P., and J. W. Johnson. 1980. Structures and Sandy Beaches. Coastal Zone '80, Hollywood Beach, Florida, November 17-20, 1980, ASCE, Vol. IV, pp. 2718-2740.

Platt, R. H. 1985. Congress and the coast. Environment 27(6):12-17, 34-39.

Platt, R. H. 1987. Coastal wetland management. Environment 29(9):16-20, 38-43.

Platt, R. H., S. G. Pelczarski, B. K. R. Burbank. 1987. Cities on the Beach: Management Issues of Developed Coastal Barriers. Research Paper No. 224. Chicago: University of Chicago Department of Geography, p. 43.

Scientific American. April 14, 1888. Moving the Brighton Beach Hotel, p. 230.

Shows, E. W. 1978. Florida's coastal setback line—an effort to regulate beach front development. Coastal Z. Mgmt. J. 4(1/2):151-164.

U.S. General Accounting Office. 1982. National Flood Insurance: Marginal Impact on Floodplain Development. CED-82-105. Washington, D.C.: General Accounting Office.

U.S. General Accounting Office. 1988. Flood Insurance: Statistics on the NFIP. GAO/RCED 88-155FS. Washington, D.C.: General Accounting Office.

4
The National
Flood Insurance Program

OVERVIEW

In the mid 1960s the federal government began to address the need for nonstructural approaches to flood loss reduction through land use planning, building/construction standards, and an insurance program. Policy makers realized that structural flood hazard controls (e.g., dams and levees) and disaster relief could not fully alleviate the nation's mounting flood losses. The financial cost of these past strategies, their environmental impacts, and their failure to do anything to minimize future flood hazards led to the conclusion that new program initiatives were needed.

Congress responded to this need by passing the National Flood Insurance Act in 1968 (P.L. 100-242, Title 13, codified at 42 USC 4001 et seq.). Key provisions of the act relevant to this study are in Appendix D of this report. This act established the National Flood Insurance Program (NFIP), with the objectives of providing affordable insurance coverage and reducing future flood losses. It required community management of new development in identified flood hazard areas consistent with minimum federal standards. The basic premise of the NFIP is clear: if communities act to limit future flood losses by instituting sound floodplain management, the government will help by assuming the financial risk faced by existing structures. Floodplain management includes, but is not limited to, building and land use regulations adopted and enforced by the local community and pursuant to national standards, established by the Federal Emergency Management Agency (FEMA). A fundamental goal of the NFIP is to be fiscally sound, namely to cover all claims out of premium income and thereby reduce future dependence on federal tax money to subsidize the program.

The act notes the importance of establishing community programs to reduce future flood loss. The National Flood Insurance Act explicitly notes that sound land use management can minimize flood losses. The act requires adoption of local land use ordinances that meet minimum federal standards as a precondition to the availability of flood insurance (see Sections 4002, 4012 in Appendix D). The general content of these minimum local management and loss prevention programs also is set out in Section 4102. A key requirement of the act and NFIP was the identification of the degree of flood hazards and risks that form the basis for the land use measures and insurance rate setting (Section 4101).

NFIP EROSION PROVISIONS

Congress explicitly dealt with the question of erosion as a flood loss in 1973, based on a finding that damage resulting from erosion and consequent undermining of structures is related in cause and is similar in effect to damage that results from floods per se. The Flood Disaster Protection Act of 1973 (P.L. 93-234, Section 107) added the following:

Section 4121 (Section 1370 of Act)

(c) "The term 'flood' shall also include the collapse or subsidence of land along the shore of a lake or other body of water as a result of erosion or undermining caused by waves or currents of water exceeding anticipated cyclical levels, and all of the provisions of this title shall apply with respect to such collapse or subsidence in the same manner and to the same extent as with respect to floods . . . including the provisions relating to land management and use. . . . " (codified at 42 U.S.C., Section 4121)

In response to this amendment, several sections were added to the NFIP regulations in 1976 to address erosion problems. First, "areas of special flood-related erosion hazards" were defined as a separate and distinct hazard area category, to be designated as "Zone E" on flood hazard maps (44 CFR, Part 65.1). Second, a statement of purpose was adopted "that all eligible communities must take into account flood, mudslide (i.e., mudflow), and flood-related erosion hazards, to the extent they are known, in all official actions relating to land management and use" (44 CFR, Part 60.1). This regulatory definition of erosion hazards is limited because it excludes erosion that occurs on a gradual scale unrelated to a flood event. Still, it did establish a framework for communities to address the problem.

The provisions for how communities are to address the erosion issue were also set forth in the 1976 addition to the regulations. Part 60.5 indicates that if a community has identified erosion as a problem in its area but has not formally established E-zones, it is required to determine, for each individual development proposal, "whether the proposed site alterations and improvements will be reasonably safe from flood-related erosion. . . ."

If an E-zone has been designated, in addition to the above requirement, the community must

"require setbacks for all new development from the ocean, lake, bay, riverfront or other body of water to create a safety buffer consisting of a natural vegetative or contour strip. This buffer will be designated by the Administrator according to the flood-related hazard and erosion rate, in conjunction with the anticipated 'useful life' of structures, and depending upon the geologic, hydrologic, topographic, and climatic characteristics of the community's land. The buffer may be used for suitable open space purposes, such as agriculture, forestry, outdoor recreation and wildlife habitat areas, and for other activities using temporary and portable structures only."

Additional sections of the regulations set out provisions for community erosion area management that are encouraged but not required. Part 60.24 encourages localities with erosion problems to direct future development to noneroding areas; to reserve erosion-prone areas for open space; to coordinate planning with neighboring communities; and to adopt preventive measures for E-zones, "including setbacks, shore protection works, relocating structures in the path of flood-related erosion, and community acquisition of flood-related erosion-prone properties for public purposes." Part 60.22 encourages adoption of postflood recovery programs to preserve open space, relocate threatened development, and acquire hazardous lands and frequently damaged properties.

Despite the inclusion of flood-related erosion hazards in the act in 1973 and the adoption of administrative regulations to address erosion hazards in 1976, the NFIP has failed in the intervening years to take action to implement these changes. No E-zones have been designated, no "safety buffers" have been designated by the administrator, and no mandatory community land use management measures for erosion hazards have been required.

EXPERIENCE WITH HAZARD DELINEATION IN THE NFIP

A great deal of time and resources have been devoted to identifying flood hazard areas under the NFIP. FEMA has initiated 12,058 detailed community flood hazard studies of which 10,799 were in effect as of October 1, 1988. The total cost of this hazard-mapping program has exceeded $800 million.

For regulatory purposes NFIP has defined its "base flood" as a flood that has a 1 percent chance of being equaled or exceeded in any given year (100-year flood). Areas subject to inundation by the base flood are called Special Flood Hazard Areas and are designated as A-zones on Flood Insurance Rate Maps (FIRMs) (see Figure 3-2).

In coastal areas V-zones (also called "coastal high-hazard areas") are designated along open coasts subject to significant wave action from hurricanes and other storms and tsunamis. V-zones usually are seaward of A-zones, which comprise the remainder of coastal areas within reach of the 1 percent flood. In practice, V-zones are areas estimated to be subject to at least a 3-foot breaking wave during a 100-year storm.

Recent regulations adopted by FEMA have included primary frontal sand dunes in the definition of V-zones (44 CFR, Part 59.1). In addition, these new regulations define criteria (44 CFR, Part 65.11) for evaluating whether a sand dune would be expected to survive intact as an effective barrier to waves and surge during a base flood event. The new definition for V-zones and the erosion criteria are to be used in areas where the extent of existing V-zones, as shown on FIRMs, underestimates the flood hazard.

Erosion is only considered in the mapping of V-zones where it affects the potential survivability of sand dunes and the height of waves during a base flood event. Long-term erosion trends are not taken into account nor are future sea level rise, subsidence, or other factors.

At the present time, V-zones have been mapped only in areas along the Atlantic and Pacific oceans and the Gulf of Mexico. However, FEMA is in the process of developing a wave runup methodology that will be used to determine and map V-zones along the Great Lakes. This remapping effort is expected to begin in 1990.

Since 1968 FEMA has gained valuable experience in floodplain management, and this program, with both its insurance and land use management components, has in many respects been the nation's primary tool for addressing development management in coastal hazard areas. Over 16,000 local governments nationally have adopted management programs that meet minimum federal standards (Godschalk et al., 1989).

Within mapped V-zones, participating communities must:

1. "Obtain the elevation (in relation to mean sea level) of the bottom of the lowest structural member of the lowest floor . . . of all new and substantially improved structures . . . and maintain a record of all such information. . . ."
2. "Provide that all new construction within V zones . . . is located landward of the reach of mean high tide."
3. "Provide that all new construction and substantial improvements . . . be elevated on pilings and columns . . . to or above the base flood level, and the pile or column foundation and structure attached thereto is anchored to resist flotation, collapse, and lateral movement. . . ."
4. "Provide that the space below the lowest floor be either free of obstruction or constructed with non-supporting breakaway walls, open wood latticework, or insect screening intended to collapse under wind and water loads. . . ."
5. "Prohibit the use of fill for structural support of buildings within V zones."
6. "Prohibit man-made alteration of sand dunes and mangrove stands within V zones which would increase potential flood damage." (44 CFR, Section 60.3)

Thus, local communities are not required to prohibit new construction or substantial improvements within V-zones, despite the high level of hazard they represent. Instead, such construction is simply required to meet certain minimum standards designed to reduce potential flood damage. No horizontal setback is required inland of mean high tide.

The committee notes several incongruities in FEMA's coastal hazards delineation. In general, V-zones are narrowly drawn. The V-zones frequently exclude adjoining areas with virtually indistinguishable hazard characteristics. The adjacent A-zones are not subject to as stringent development controls as the V-zones. In Newport Beach, California, for instance, the boundary between ZONE VE (EL 11) and ZONE AE (EL 11) runs down the middle of the beach in places. However, within ZONE AE commercial development may be constructed at grade level if floodproofed to 11 feet (i.e., base flood elevation). In the VE zone, it must be elevated on pilings to that level.

There is also disparity in requirements regarding V-zones in contrast with riverine floodways. A floodway is defined as "the channel of a river or other watercourse and the adjacent land areas that must be reserved in order to discharge the base flood without cumulatively increasing the water surface elevation more than [1 foot]." Within designated floodways, the community must "prohibit encroachment, including fill, new construction, substantial improvements, and other development within the adopted regulatory floodway that would result in any increase in flood levels within the community during the occurrence of the base flood discharge" (44 CFR, Section 60.3(d)(3)). Although the concept of restricting development of the floodway deals with increasing the hazard for others, the regulations have the effect of restricting development in areas of the floodplain that are normally deeper and with higher velocities and thus more hazardous. New construction virtually is prohibited within floodways. Such restrictions do not apply in the most hazardous open-coast areas. Development may and widely does occur in V-zones. The failure to identify a comparable area of highest hazard (both in terms of potential for damage to structures located within such areas and in terms of their contribution to increasing the hazards to other structures from their floating debris in storms) is of serious concern, particularly given the potential for future coastal erosion.

Another concern is the infrequency of map updates. Given the high cost of individual map preparation, the experience in flood hazard mapping has been to remap on an average frequency of once every 9 years. In addition to these full reviews, FEMA has completed numerous minor map revisions, either physical map revisions or letter amendments, more frequently. In highly dynamic coastal areas, particularly those with severe erosion problems, such infrequent remapping could cause hazards to be seriously underestimated. Perhaps a Geographic Information System (GIS) system could be used to facilitate revisions to coastal maps.

EXPERIENCE WITH COSTS

Several factors in the early years of NFIP implementation delayed realization of the expected cost savings relative to structural controls and disaster relief (Houck, 1985). Detailed and costly maps of flood hazard areas had to be prepared. During the detailed mapping process, property owners in participating communities were allowed to obtain a limited amount of insurance, even though the full program development management ordinances were not in place. Insurance rates were subsidized to secure widespread property owner participation. As a result, the flood insurance program paid $651.6

million more in claims than was received in premiums during the 1978-1987 period (General Accounting Office, 1988). When the costs of hazard mapping and administration are considered, the governmental costs of this program are even higher. For example, FEMA reported that for 1987 alone, its costs that were not included in the charges against premiums totaled $54.5 million (including $36.5 million for flood studies and hazard mapping) (FEMA, 12/28/87).

These trends have been reversed in recent years. Most of the initial detailed flood hazard mapping has been completed. Approximately 2.1 million policies with $162 billion in coverage were in effect on December 31, 1987 (General Accounting Office, 1988). The policies in force generated an estimated $481.3 million in insurance premiums in 1987 (General Accounting Office, 1988). Over 16,500 communities have adopted full "regular program" status floodplain ordinances that meet minimum federal standards. In addition, insurance premium rates have doubled since 1981, bringing the NFIP closer to being actuarially sound and self-supporting.

As of August 31, 1987, V-zones that are often synonymous with areas subject to erosion hazards accounted for 64,000 policies (3.1 percent of NFIP total) and $5.2 billion in total coverage (3.3 percent of NFIP total). The average annual premium charge in V zones was $469, in comparison with $259 for the program as a whole (General Accounting Office, 1988).

NFIP losses for V-zones totaled 11,253 claims for the period January 1, 1978, through September 30, 1988 (3.3 percent of NFIP total). These losses totaled $92.9 million paid to insured property owners compared to total premium revenue from V-zone policies of approximately $138 million during that same period. The average amount of loss in V-zones was $8,260, slightly higher than $7,069 for the program as a whole. V-zone policies also accounted for 3,000 repetitive losses totaling $24.4 million during this same time period, amounting to about 2 percent of program totals for this category (General Accounting Office, 1988).

To date, V-zone policies have paid their own way and have not generated excessive or unacceptable numbers of losses or repetitive losses. The foregoing data, however, may well provide a misleading picture of the potential liability to the NFIP posed by coverage in V-zones. Hurricane Hugo in 1989, the first category 4 hurricane since Camille in 1969, will result in revision of estimates of flooding zones on the Atlantic coast. Much of the coverage in V-zones applies to structures built since the occurrence of the most recent hurricane in that locality but prior to current NFIP elevation requirements. Furthermore, all V-zone structures on eroding shorelines are subject to rising levels of risk due to major storms.

FEMA's experience suggests that older structures not built to the more stringent building standards will suffer greater losses. For example, the 1978-1987 average operating surplus per policy for pre-FIRM structures in V-zones was only $12.97, compared to $185.22 for similar post-FIRM structures (Federal Emergency Management Agency, 1988). The stage therefore is set for major losses to V-zone property (as well as the neighboring A-, B- and C-zone property) in the event of a major storm in the future. Most significantly, the level of risk to existing development in V-zones (as well as in other zones near coastlines of the oceans, Gulf of Mexico, and the Great Lakes) is increasing along eroding shorelines.

LOSS PREVENTION UNDER THE NFIP: THE UPTON-JONES AMENDMENT

In 1987 Congress became concerned over the ever-increasing number of structures threatened by coastal erosion. Rising water levels in the Great Lakes threatened to undermine the trend toward fiscal integrity for the NFIP and become a serious drain on other federal fiscal resources.

Much attention has been focused on managing the location and construction of new coastal development. A 1986 survey of coastal states indicated that 19 of 23 responding states were involved in managing new development in coastal natural hazard areas through setbacks, construction standards, and/or land use controls (Coastal States Organization, 1986). (See Chapter 5 for a detailed review of some of these management programs.) However, little attention had been given to addressing problems of existing development that is increasingly at risk as shorelines continue to retreat. In view of the number of flood insurance policies in coastal areas and their exposure to loss, this concern was well placed. In response to these concerns, the Upton-Jones Amendment (Section 544, Housing and Community Development Act of 1987, see Appendix A) was enacted into law.

The Upton-Jones Amendment was proposed by Representative Fred Upton (R-Michigan) in the spring of 1987. Abnormally high water levels in the Great Lakes had destroyed a large number of structures. Many houses literally fell over eroding bluffs into the lakes, creating debris and safety problems for neighbors and local governments. To assist these beleaguered communities, Representative Upton proposed allowing flood insurance loss payments to be made after threatened structures were condemned but before they actually collapsed. Payments of 110 percent of the insured value would be authorized, with the extra 10 percent covering the cost of demolition and debris removal.

When the Housing Act containing this amendment was being considered by the House of Representatives in the summer of 1987, Representative Walter Jones (D-North Carolina) proposed a floor amendment to include coverage of the costs of relocating structures endangered by coastal erosion. Although minimum ocean-front setbacks had been imposed by his home state in 1979, an ever-increasing number of existing beach cottages in North Carolina were facing eventual collapse into the sea. In 1986 the state estimated that in North Carolina alone some 750 ocean-front structures insured at an estimated $50.6 million would be lost to erosion in the next 10 years, with the number rising to some 5,000 structures potentially being lost over a 60-year period. Further, some 4,200 of these structures, insured at an estimated $314.5 million, were predicted to be at immediate risk in the event of a major coastal storm (Division of Coastal Management, Department of Natural Resources and Community Development, 1986). Faced with these potential losses, Representative Jones proposed avoiding these near-certain 100 percent losses by paying up to 40 percent of the insured value for the purposes of relocating the endangered structures to safer locations.

The combined amendment, commonly called the Upton-Jones Amendment, was adopted unanimously by the House of Representatives on June 11, 1987. It was incorporated with modest revisions by the conference committee into the final version of the Housing and Community Development Act adopted by the full Congress in December 1987 and was signed into law by the President on February 5, 1988.

Prior to the Upton-Jones Amendment, NFIP paid claims only on insured buildings that had actually sustained physical damage as a result of flooding or flood-related erosion. The amendment allows for the payment of a claim prior to actual damage for the purpose of relocating or demolishing the structure. For purposes of a claim payment under the amendment, the value of the structure is determined by the lowest of the following:

• the value of a comparable structure that is not subject to imminent collapse;

- the price paid for the structure and any improvement to the structure, adjusted for inflation; or
- the value of the structure under the flood insurance contract.

Compensation up to the allowable limits, as applicable, is included for removing the structure from the site, site cleanup, debris removal, moving the structure to a new site, and, at the new site, construction of a new foundation and related grading and utility connections. There is no compensation for land values, sheds, fences, walls, and driveways. The cost of purchasing additional property, if needed, is the responsibility of the insured.

To be eligible for a claim payment, the structure must have been covered by a contract of flood insurance on or before June 1, 1988, for a period of 2 years, or for the term of ownership if less than 2 years. The structure also must be subject to imminent collapse as a result of erosion or undermining caused by waves or currents of water exceeding anticipated cyclical levels.

In making imminent collapse determinations, FEMA has adopted interim criteria based on a setback from the shoreline. Specifically, the building must be located within a zone defined as an area seaward of a line that is 10 feet plus five times the local average annual shoreline recession rate as measured from a prominent physical reference feature, such as the edge of a bluff or dune escarpment or the normal high-water limit. The normal high-water limit may be indicated by a line of permanent vegetation, a sharp escarpment on the beach, a debris line deposited by the normal tide, or the upper limit of wet sand. For structures that fall outside this zone, FEMA will consider any technical or scientific data submitted with the claim that demonstrates a unique or highly unstable condition at the site.

Once FEMA has approved a determination of imminent collapse on a property, future flood insurance coverage and certain types of federal disaster assistance will be available only for buildings on that property that are constructed or relocated beyond the area that is expected to erode within the next 30 years (i.e., 30-year setback) for one- to four-family dwellings. All other buildings must be located beyond the area expected to erode within the next 60 years (i.e., 60-year setback) in order to be insurable under the NFIP. Structures that are relocated to a different property also must meet these setback standards for future insurance coverage availability. In addition, relocated structures must comply as well with minimum floodplain management regulations such as elevating or floodproofing to the base flood elevation if the new site is in a designated Special Flood

Hazard Area. Owners of structures that are not relocated or demolished within a reasonable amount of time following a determination of imminent collapse by FEMA will be eligible to recover only 40 percent of their covered losses should the structure be damaged subsequently by a flood.

The amendment directs FEMA to issue regulations defining criteria and procedures whereby state and local governments may certify that a structure is subject to imminent collapse as a result of erosion or undermining caused by waves or currents of water exceeding anticipated cyclical levels. This certification process replaces the interim condemnation requirement now operating that varies widely among municipalities. To bridge the gap between condemnation and the issuance of a final rule for a state and local certification process, FEMA has published an interim rule (44 CFR, Part 63, Subpart B) for state certification. States are eligible for this interim certification process if they meet certain qualifications. These qualifications include

- the existence of a statewide coastal zone setback program;
- the existence of data on long-term shoreline recession rates developed for the state's coastal shorelines; and
- a setback standard that is based, at least in part, on a multiple of the local shoreline recession rate.

States that have applied for and been approved to make certifications to date include, with date of approval indicated parenthetically, North Carolina (10/13/88), Michigan (2/8/89), South Carolina (3/2/89), and Pennsylvania (3/2/89).

States that qualify for this interim certification process are required to collect data and information demonstrating that the structure is within a zone near the shoreline (i.e., 10 feet plus five times the recession rate) or otherwise is in an area that is unique or highly unstable, rendering the structure subject to imminent collapse. These data and information are reviewed by FEMA when a claim is filed by the insured in making a determination of imminent collapse. The final rule will further define the qualification requirements for both state and local governments and the criteria and procedure for issuance of a certification of imminent collapse.

In addition to the statutory provisions in the amendment, the accompanying conference committee report for the housing act approved by Congress (Report 100-426) urged FEMA to take additional steps to address the problems of future losses caused by coastal erosion. Specifically, FEMA was asked to consider requiring adequate land use management controls related to erosion as a precondition for community participation in the NFIP and to adjust insurance premiums to include an erosion rate factor. The conference report refers to the existing authorities under Section 4022 (Section 1315 of Act), which states:

". . . no new flood insurance coverage shall be provided under this title in any area (or subdivision thereof) unless an appropriate public body shall have adopted adequate land use and control measures (with effective enforcement provisions) which the [Director of FEMA] finds are consistent with the comprehensive criteria for land management and use under section 1361."

Section 4102 (Section 1361 of Act) states:

(a) "The [Director of FEMA] is authorized to carry out studies and investigations . . . with respect to the adequacy of State and local measures in flood-prone areas as to the land management and use, flood control, flood zoning and flood damage prevention. . . ."

(b) "Such studies and investigations shall include, but not be limited to, laws, regulations, or ordinances relating to encroachments and obstructions on stream channels and floodways, the orderly development and use of flood plains of rivers or streams, floodway encroachment lines, and flood plain zoning, building codes, building permits, and subdivision or other building restrictions."

The conference committee report also indicated that "in order to effectively implement the erosion setback requirements, FEMA will be required to develop and publish tables of annual erosion rates for the calculation of erosion setbacks" and referred to Section 1361 as containing the necessary authorities to conduct such studies.

Since the Upton-Jones Amendment originated as a House floor amendment to a Senate-passed act, the conference committee had limited ability to address additional issues and questions raised about the provisions and its impacts during its deliberations. Issues discussed at that time included whether title to the land being vacated by a relocated or demolished structure should remain with the original owner or be acquired by the public, either in fee or in the form of an open-space easement (perhaps combining the relocation program with the Section 1362 property acquisition program). Another question was the adequacy of the minimum setbacks, with 50 and 100 years being suggested as potential alternatives to the 30- and 60-year provisions in the law. Also discussed was the adequacy of sanctions for owners who fail to take appropriate loss prevention steps, such as cancellation of flood insurance and disaster relief. Finally, the substance of a minimum state or local erosion area management program was also discussed, as was its relation to the postdisaster mitigation plans prepared under Section 406 of the Disaster Relief Act and implementation of the FEMA regulations on special erosion hazard areas (i.e., zone E). Several of these issues were discussed in the conference report, but many were held over for resolution when Congress considers extension of this program after a 2-year trial.

On January 3, 1989, Congressmen Jones and Upton introduced legislation to extend this program for 2 additional years and to make several technical changes in its provisions (H.R. 236). These changes included clarifying that the requirement to take mitigative action or face reduction of future flood insurance benefits is triggered upon a certification of imminent collapse rather than submission of a claim by the property owner. As of fall 1989 Congress was considering an extension without change of the Upton-Jones provision as part of a 2-year extension of the overall NFIP.

EXPERIENCE TO DATE WITH THE
UPTON-JONES AMENDMENT

As of August 28, 1989, experience with the implementation of the loss prevention provisions included in the NFIP by the Upton-Jones Amendment has been very limited. Approximately 29 percent of these claims were for structures located in noncoastal settings (i.e., riverine) since the amendment specifically includes all "bodies of water." It is somewhat surprising that only 266 claims had been filed since the amendment was enacted into law on February 5, 1988, particularly in view of the estimates on the number of threatened structures in North Carolina and Michigan, which account for 41 percent of all claims and 58 percent of the coastal claims (Table 4-1). The relatively high number of claims from North Carolina (81) is attributed in part to a March 1989 storm that caused significant beach and dune erosion in the Nags Head area. Many of the structures in these claims sustained significant damage during this event and were beyond repair. It should be noted that these figures do not include any claims resulting from Hurricane Hugo's impact on the South Carolina/North Carolina coast in September 1989. Preliminary reports indicate that over 350 Upton-Jones claims may result in North Carolina with a substantially larger number expected from South Carolina.

The overall low response to the coverage and benefits provided

TABLE 4-1 Upton-Jones Claims Summary (August 28, 1989)

Total Claims Filed	266
Relocation	77
Demolition	143
Unknown	46
Approved for payment	
(average $47,109)	86
Demolition	70
Relocation	16
Claims denied	92
Withdrawn	24
Pending	64
Coastal Claims	188
(Average age of structure	32 years)
Delaware	1
Florida	5
Maryland	1
North Carolina	81
Ohio	11
Texas	9
Massachusetts	21
Michigan	29
New York	2
Pennsylvania	19
Virginia	7
South Carolina	2
Coastal claims approved	74
(Average age of structure	33 years)
(Average amount approved	$49,601)
Relocation	14
(Average age of structure	22 years)
(Average amount	$25,455)
Demolition	60
(Average age of structure	35 years)
(Average amount	$55,235)
Coastal claims denied	45
No condemnation, in AEZ	23
Condemned, not in AEZ	2
No condemnation and not in AEZ	15
Other	5
Coastal Claims Withdrawn	16
Coastal Claims Pending	53

by the Upton-Jones Amendment could be attributed to a number of reasons, including the following:

1. The requirement of sufficient actual structural damage to warrant condemnation of the structure, a requirement in place for most states prior to early 1989 (and remaining in effect for all but four states as of October 1989).
2. Lack of awareness of the changes in coverage and the procedures for filing a claim (although FEMA has indicated that each policy holder was sent a notice of change in their policy).
3. Reluctance to remove or interrupt income from rental property.
4. Lack of suitable and affordable alternate property for relocation.
5. Lower Great Lakes water levels in the past 2 years have provided some relief from the threat of damage.
6. The lack of coverage for the cost of land acquisition for relocation sites.

It is interesting to note that 24 (16 coastal) claims were withdrawn. According to FEMA, these claims were withdrawn for a variety of reasons, including the following: the appraised value of the structure was lower than expected, the house fell into the ocean, the house was sold, and the claim was submitted as a casual inquiry. In addition, coverage for actual damages, should they occur, would still be covered in the event of flooding or flood-related erosion for the replacement cost, which may be higher than the "actual cash value" criteria used in a claim filed under the Upton-Jones Amendment.

Demolition is the favored option, accounting for approximately two out of three claims filed and four out of five claims approved, a factor likely related to the condemnation requirement. The average value of settlement on approved claims for relocation and demolition claims has been $47,109 for all claims and $49,601 for coastal claims. The average approved settlement amount on coastal claims for demolition ($55,235) is more than twice the amount for relocation ($25,455).

Of the 45 coastal claims that have been denied, the primary reason was lack of a condemnation notice (23 of the 45). Fifteen of the structures for these claims were also found to be outside the "active erosion zone." It is noted that the average age of structures for approved coastal claims was 33 years, with those preferring the demolition option 13 years older (35 years) than those preferring the relocation option (22 years). Finally, 53 of the 188 coastal claims filed as of August 28, 1989, are still pending.

It should be noted that these statistics are very preliminary in nature and have limited applicability to a full-scale relocation initiative. This is primarily due to the lack of implementation of the relocation option without a condemnation prerequisite.

The Upton-Jones Amendment adds an important new capability to the NFIP. For the first time, benefits are available to insured property owners before an actual loss occurs, provided steps are taken to prevent a subsequent larger loss. The opportunity thus is provided for structures to be removed from erosion-prone locations—by demolition or relocation—in an orderly manner and with minimum threat to public safety or private investment. This anticipatory approach should help reduce public and private costs related to erosion.

The Upton-Jones Amendment is a tentative step in the direction of a strategy that emphasizes retreat from eroding shorelines. This approach represents an appropriate means for reducing NFIP loss payments and promoting public coastal management objectives. But so far the Upton-Jones Amendment has had modest influence on the owners of property at risk from erosion. Only 266 claims had been filed as of August 28, 1989 (Table 4-1). This is a modest number in comparison with the total number of coastal structures threatened by erosion. In North Carolina alone it is estimated that 4,200 structures are within the 100-year average annual erosion rate (AAER) zone, of which 777 are within the 10-year AAER zone (response of the North Carolina Department of Natural Resources and Community Development to the Association of State Floodplain Managers [ASFPM] Survey, September 1988). While North Carolina is not typical of all coastal states (there is no "typical" state), this example makes it clear that the provisions of Upton-Jones are not yet being taken advantage of by the owners of a large segment of insured structures threatened by erosion.

The limited response to Upton-Jones to date apparently has resulted in part from a narrow reading by FEMA of the statutory language regarding eligibility for benefits under the amendment. Section 544 (amending Section 1306(c) of the National Flood Insurance Act) states that the provision applies to insured structures that are certified by an appropriate state or local land use authority to be:

". . . subject to imminent collapse or subsidence as a result of erosion or undermining caused by waves or currents of water exceeding anticipated cyclical levels. . . ."

FEMA in its interim regulations issued September 23, 1988, defines "zone of imminent collapse" to mean

". . . an area subject to erosion adjacent to the shoreline of an ocean, bay, or lake and within a distance equal to 10 feet plus 5 times the average annual long-term erosion rate for the site, measured from the reference feature."

If the intent of Congress is that the Upton-Jones Amendment be used to encourage anticipatory action to remove structures threatened by erosion, then FEMA's interim definition of "zone of imminent collapse" is too narrow and restrictive to accomplish this. For shorelines experiencing an AAER of 1 to 2 feet, a structure would need to be within 15 to 20 feet of the "reference feature" (e.g., frontal edge of bluff or dune, normal high-water line, or seaward line of vegetation) before it could be certified to be eligible for Upton-Jones benefits. Such a narrow zone of eligibility leaves little margin of error for miscalculation of the AAER, mislocation of the reference feature, or trust that a large storm event will not soon occur.

Furthermore, the occurrence of a major storm (such as Hurricane Hugo) causing severe erosion would jeopardize many structures in this narrow zone and render their subsequent orderly relocation or demolition infeasible. The narrow definition of "zone of imminent collapse" (see Figure 4-1) adopted by FEMA thus defeats the objectives of the Upton-Jones Amendment by forcing property owners to wait until orderly removal may be impossible before structures can be certified as imminently endangered. The definition reflects an unrealistic level of confidence in our ability to estimate exact AAER rates and to identify appropriate reference features in the field. A larger margin of error is needed to afford more time to relocate threatened structures. This is the basis for the committee's recommendation that FEMA expand its definition of "zone of imminent collapse" at least to a distance of 10 times the long-term AAER.

Following are other considerations that would improve the effectiveness of the Upton-Jones element of the NFIP:

- Relocation should be encouraged in preference to demolition wherever feasible.
- Structures being relocated pursuant to Upton-Jones should be required to be relocated landward of the E-30 line. Section 544 prohibits the availability of flood insurance or federal disaster assistance to relocated structures that do not meet that test. The statute suggests that FEMA may deny an Upton-Jones payment to struc-

88

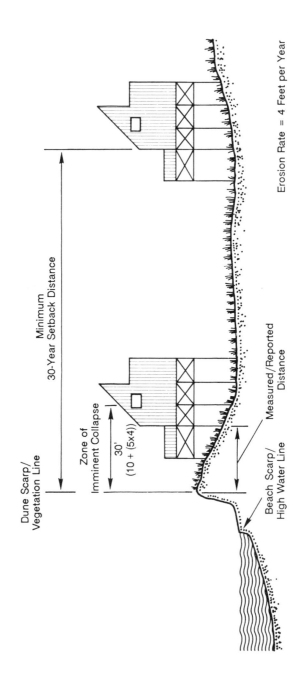

FIGURE 4-1 FEMA's criteria for imminent collapse and setback determinations under the Upton-Jones Amendment.

tures that are not relocated landward sufficiently to at least gain protection for an estimated period of 30 years.

• FEMA should require as a condition to any payment under Section 544 that the vacated site be legally restricted (preferably through a recorded easement) against any reuse involving an enclosed and habitable structure, whether or not it is covered by a flood insurance policy. Such an easement would not involve public access but would permanently divest any right to obtain a building permit for rebuilding on the vacated site.

• After a structure is certified as being within the "zone of imminent collapse" and after proper notification of the owner, FEMA should terminate insurance coverage of the structure under the NFIP or substantially increase the premium if relocation or demolition does not occur within a reasonable period of time.

• Care should be exercised by FEMA to assure the compatibility of new erosion-related development standards with the existing flood-related construction standards.

• An appeal procedure should be established by FEMA whereby aggrieved property owners may challenge a presumption that erosion is continuing at the estimated rate.

DELINEATION AND LOCAL MANAGEMENT OF E-ZONES

FEMA has not yet designated any erosion hazard zones (E-zones) or established national standards for setbacks or other management requirements for erosion-prone coasts under 44 CFR, Section 60.5. As discussed in Chapter 5, about 11 states have independently established setback regulations based on estimates of long-term AAERs or some other criterion.

Now that FEMA is mandated by the Upton-Jones Amendment to facilitate retreat from eroding shores, through insurance claim payments for relocation or demolition of buildings subject to imminent collapse, it is essential that it address the need for comprehensive approaches to the management of erosion-prone areas within communities participating in the NFIP. Upton-Jones was meant to be a first step toward a broader FEMA role as stated by Representative Walter B. Jones:

"The Amendment does not constrain FEMA from taking additional steps to further reduce the hazards related to erosion. . . . The section should be viewed as an important first step in dealing with the problem of erosion, and FEMA should be encouraged to take additional actions to fully utilize its existing authorities to address this problem on a broader scale." (*Federal Register*, November 19, 1987, P.E. 4547)

FEMA needs to implement 44 CFR, Section 60.5, to establish E-zones and set appropriate minimum standards for management of land use within such zones by communities participating in the NFIP. Such requirements would augment and not replace existing floodplain management standards.

E-zones should encompass areas along eroding coasts to a landward limit equivalent to an E-60 line (see Chapter 6 for the methodology for setting this line). The foregoing limits correspond to those in the Upton-Jones Amendment and are used in several states, notably North Carolina and Michigan.

However, FEMA should, through education and insurance rate setting, encourage communities to require a more restrictive setback—for example, a 50-year AAER for small structures and 100-year AAER for larger ones. Communities could be encouraged to exceed the FEMA minimum by offering reduced premiums for NFIP insurance coverage.

In 1987 FEMA began to formulate a new approach to community flood hazard management. Under the proposed Community Rating System (CRS), communities that exceed minimum NFIP floodplain management standards would be rewarded with credits toward reduced premium rates communitywide. Two of the activities that would be "credited" by CRS would be "acquiring additional data" and imposing "higher regulatory standards."

If CRS is implemented, coastal communities should be encouraged by FEMA to acquire additional erosion data and to impose stronger limits on new construction. Specifically, communities should be rewarded by CRS if they adopt setbacks of E-50 for small structures and E-100 for large ones, in place of the minimum standards of E-30 and E-60 proposed in this report.

FEMA should incorporate state and other existing erosion rate data that conform with federal technical standards wherever justified (see Chapter 6 for details). There is no reason to undertake independent federal studies of erosion rates where the state already has a good data base and program for monitoring ongoing erosion. State AAER data may be used directly in the designation of E-zones.

When E-zones are designated, FEMA should implement 44 CFR, Section 60.5, so that state or local government shall require a setback for all new development from the ocean, lake, bay, or other body of water to create a safety buffer consisting of a natural vegetative or contour strip. All new construction (except water-dependent structures, such as docks and piers) should be located landward of the established setbacks. These recommended setbacks are (1) between the water and the E-10 line, no habitable structures; (2) between the E-10 and E-30 lines, only readily movable single-family dwellings, and these only if the E-30 setback cannot be met on a preexisting lot and this limited development is allowed by a state or local variance; (3) between the E-30 and E-60 lines, any readily movable structures; and (4) large structures (e.g., those more than 5,000 square feet) landward of the E-60 line.

In addition, FEMA should consider imposing a premium surcharge on existing structures within an E-zone that are insured under the NFIP to be used to finance necessary relocations and higher expected loss rates. Structures within the "zone of imminent collapse" (10-year AAER as suggested herein) would be subject to substantial annual increases in this surcharge or, at the option of FEMA, termination of coverage within a reasonable time after notification of the property owner of eligibility for Upton-Jones benefits. The latter consideration requires legislative action.

Finally, FEMA should decline to insure new structures or substantial improvements within E-10 zones. This would require legislative action. Currently, there are about 64,000 NFIP policies in V-zones totaling $5.2 billion in coverage. E-10 zones by definition are areas of imminent hazard and represent a nonactuarial risk. Coverage of new structures on the open coast in areas exposed to both flood and erosion hazards encourages undesirable building practices.

Hurricane Hugo, which hit the South Carolina coast in late September 1989, caused major destruction and loss of property. According to the Federal Insurance Administration, preliminary estimates for the total payment on all claims for flood damage resulting from Hurricane Hugo will be between $225 million and $275 million. At this time, the flood insurance fund generated from premium income is sufficient to pay this amount, and there will be no need to rely on tax dollars to compensate those who have suffered flood damage.

INCLUSION OF EROSION IN UNIFIED NATIONAL PROGRAM

Section 1302(c) of the National Flood Insurance Act states that ". . . the objectives of a flood insurance program should be inte-

grally related to a unified national program for flood plain management. . . ." Pursuant to this mandate, a document entitled *A Unified
National Program for Floodplain Management* was first published by
the U.S. Water Resources Council at the direction of the Office of
Management and Budget in 1977. This document was revised in
1979 to reflect Executive Orders 11988 and 11990 concerned respectively with flood hazards and wetlands. With the termination of the
Water Resources Council in 1981, responsibility for updating and
implementing the unified program shifted to FEMA, which issued a
further revised version in March 1986.

The unified program in its current form articulates a framework
for achieving floodplain management objectives through cooperative
use of a broad range of existing institutional and legislative arrange-
ments at the federal, regional, state, and local levels of government.
Coordination of relevant federal agencies having authority over aspects of land use in flood hazard areas is pursued through a federal
interagency task force for flood loss reduction with FEMA as the
lead agency. In this matter FEMA seeks to reinforce its flood loss
reduction efforts under the NFIP by collaborating with agencies that
exercise public works, regulatory, or other statutory functions in
floodplains.

The unified program, however, lacks any component that addresses erosion hazards. There is no explicit discussion of the role of
erosion as a contributing factor in exacerbating coastal flood losses.
Nor is the occurrence of erosion outside designated flood hazard
zones addressed (e.g., from bluff undermining and collapse). There
is no consideration of the interaction of shoreline protection activities, either "hard" or "soft," with the natural processes of beach
formation and erosion. And the use of setbacks, relocation, and
other nonstructural responses to erosion-related flood hazards is not
discussed.

FEMA should revise the *Unified National Program for Floodplain Management* to include erosion hazards along the nation's
coasts. This discussion should address the nature of erosion both as
a contributing factor in flood losses and as an independent hazard.
The pros and cons of alternative forms of public response should
be reviewed. The respective roles and responsibilities of the federal,
state, and local levels of government should be articulated in parallel
with the present treatment of flood hazards.

FEMA also should convene a special task force on coastal erosion management. This body would include experts from federal

agencies and universities having policy or program responsibilities affecting coastal erosion—for example, FEMA, the Army Corps of Engineers, the Environmental Protection Agency, the Department of the Interior (U.S. Geological Survey and National Park Service), and NOAA (Office of Ocean and Coastal Resource Management). Experts from states with critical erosion problems and/or significant coastal erosion management programs should be invited to participate in the task force. The purposes of the task force would include the following:

• Assist FEMA in developing and promulgating a nationwide standard for erosion hazard reduction equivalent to the 100-year flood standard.

• Review internal procedures of participating agencies to determine compatibility with erosion management provisions of the *Unified National Program* (as revised).

• Review the applicability of Executive Orders 11988 and 11990 to the management of erosion hazards and, if appropriate, recommend revisions thereof to the President.

• Serve as an ongoing technical advisory committee concerning coastal erosion with the capability of commissioning special studies and research projects where appropriate to further goals of the *Unified National Program.*

REFERENCES

Coastal States Organization. 1986. Coastal Hazard Reduction Survey.

Division of Coastal Management, Department of Natural Resources and Community Development. 1986. North Carolina Threatened Structure Survey. Document I&S 173(a) and North Carolina National Flood Insurance Program Case Study. Document I&S 174 (b).

Federal Emergency Management Agency. 1988. Various handouts and memos to the committee.

General Accounting Office. 1988. Flood Insurance: Statistics on the National Flood Insurance Program. April.

Godschalk, D., D. Brower, and T. Beatley. 1989. Catastrophic Coastal Storms: Hazard Mitigation and Development Management.

Houck, O. A. 1985. Rising water: The National Flood Insurance Program and Louisiana. Tulane L. Rev. 60:61.

5

State Programs and Experiences

TYPES OF STATE PROGRAMS

Only about one-third of the water-boundary (coastal) states have active erosion hazard area management programs that include the establishment of erosion setbacks for new construction (Table 5-1). However, it is noteworthy that several states have general setback requirements that, while not based on erosion hazards, have the effect of limiting construction near the shoreline.

About two-thirds of the states measure the rate of recession (erosion) with the use of aerial photographs. Besides being used for state regulation, recession rates are useful in providing information and education to property owners and in support of local government regulations. The absence of erosion hazard area programs in most states can be attributed to a lack of erosion, lack of development, reliance on shore protection to control upland erosion, and other factors. Some states presently are considering erosion-based setback requirements or recently have implemented them.

Program Elements

Coastal states have gained considerable experience in the implementation and administration of regulatory erosion programs.

Nineteen of twenty-three states responding to a Coastal States Organization survey conducted by the state of North Carolina in 1986 indicated they use direct regulatory authority to mitigate damage from coastal hazards. The survey found that about 82 percent of the responding states have regulations to mitigate coastal hazards, including erosion, flooding, storm surge, and so on. The Association of State Floodplain Managers Survey of 1988 found that about 33 percent of the states had a regulatory program specifically addressing erosion hazard management.

Erosion hazard zones often have been delineated, in conjunction with university and consulting specialists. Each state has developed slightly different regulations in hazard areas. This appears to be based on the language of the law being enacted; the geomorphology of the coast; and the result of discretionary decisions, such as the threshold rate of recession, the years of setback protection, and other locally decided variables.

Most states with setback regulatory programs use the local unit of government to administer the program, either on a mandatory or voluntary basis. In most instances the local unit of government is given latitude in formulating local regulations. This allows the local unit of government to retain control of its land use activities and exceed the minimum state requirements, if it desires.

Technical standards also vary from state to state. Most states with regulatory programs have established a threshold erosion standard of 1 foot per year to define a high hazard area. Some states have established setback requirements along all erodible shores because even small erosion losses can threaten homes constructed too close to the shoreline.

State and local governments employ several techniques to transform recession rate data into hazard zones with specific setback requirements. Many state programs employ data averaging or "grouping" procedures. Grouping involves placing recession rates that are similar in magnitude (usually defined as a variation from a mean value) in a common pool. The rates then are averaged for the length of shoreline. The process results in a single value being assigned as the representative recession rate for a length of shoreline. Some states establish only one setback standard per local unit of government. Likewise, local units of government sometimes adopt the highest setback in the community as the standard throughout the community for ease of administration. Some states require different setbacks for different classes of buildings, such as a 30-year setback

TABLE 5-1 Summary of State and Territory Erosion Management Programs

State/Territory	Recession Rates from Aerial Photos	Recession Rates from Charts	Recession Rates from Ground Surveys	Erosion Setbacks Established*	Reference Feature	Years of Setback	Local Administration	One Foot per Year Standard	Fixed Setback	Floating Setback
Alabama	Y	Y	N	Y	MHW	NA	N	Y	N	NA
Alaska	Y	Y		N	NA	NA	NA	NA	NA	NA
American Samoa	N	N	N	N	NA	NA	NA	NA	NA	NA
California	Y	Y	Y	N	NA	NA	Y	NA	NA	NA
Connecticut	Y	Y		N	NA	NA	NA	NA	NA	NA
Delaware	Y	Y		Y4	TD	NA	Y	N	Y	N
Florida	Y	Y		Y5	NA	30	Y	N	Y	N
Georgia	Y	Y		N	NA	NA	Y	NA	NA	NA
Hawaii	N	N	N	Y	6	N	Y	N	Y	N
Indiana	Y	N	Y	N	NA	NA	NA	Y	NA	NA
Illinois	Y	Y	Y	N	NA	NA	NA		NA	NA
Louisiana	Y	Y	N	N	NA	NA	NA	NA	NA	NA
Maine	N	N	Y	N7	NA	NA	NA	NA	NA	NA
Maryland	Y	Y		N	NA	NA	NA	NA	NA	NA
Massachusetts	Y	Y	N	N	NA	NA	NA	NA	NA	NA
Michigan	Y	N	N	Y	BC2	30	Y	Y	N	Y
Minnesota	Y	N	N	N	NA	NA	NA	Y	N	NA
Mississippi	N	N	N	N	NA	NA	NA	Y	NA	NA
New Hampshire	N	N	N	N	NA	NA	NA	NA	NA	NA
New Jersey	Y	Y	Y	Y	MHW	50	NA	NA	NA	NA

TABLE 5-1 Continued

State/Territory	Recession Rates from Aerial Photos	Recession Rates from Charts	Recession Rates from Ground Surveys	Erosion Setbacks Established*	Reference Feature	Years of Setback	Local Administration	One Foot per Year Standard	Fixed Setback	Floating Setback
New York	Y	Y	N	Y	BC	30-40	Y	Y	Y	N
North Carolina	Y	N		Y	DC	30-60	Y	N	N	Y
N. Mariana's	N	N	N	Y	NA	NA	NA	NA	NA	NA
Ohio	Y	Y	N	N1	BC	30	NA	Y	Y	N
Oregon				N		NA	NA	NA	NA	NA
Pennsylvania	Y	N	Y	Y	BC	50+	Y	Y	N	Y
Puerto Rico	N	N	N	N	NA	NA	NA	NA	N	
Rhode Island	N	N	Y	Y	DC	30	N	N7	Y	N
South Carolina			Y	Y		40	BL		Y	N
Texas	Y	Y	Y	N	NA	NA	NA	NA	NA	NA
Virgin Islands	N	N	N	N	NA	NA	NA	NA	NA	NA
Virginia	Y	Y		N	MHW	NA	Y			
Washington					NA	NA	NA	NA	NA	NA
Wisconsin	Y	Y	N	N3	NA	NA	NA	NA	N	Y

NOTE: 1 = setbacks may be established within 2 years; 2 = bluff crest or edge of active erosion; 3 = some counties have setbacks; 4 = has 100 foot setback regulation over new subdivisions and parcels where sufficient room exists landward of setback; 5 = not all counties have coastal construction control lines established; 6 = storm debris line or vegetation line; 7 = 2 feet per year standard. Y, yes; N, no; NA, not applicable; BC, bluff crest; MHW, mean high water; TD, toe of dune; DC, dune crest, toe of frontal dune or vegetation line; BL, base line. A blank means no information was available.

*Most states have setbacks from water line but not based on an erosion hazard.

for single-family structures, a 60-year setback for multiple-family structures, and a 100-year setback for industrial buildings.

The point from which the setback is measured is broadly termed the "reference feature." The reference feature varies from state to state but relies heavily on the geomorphic character of the area. In cliff or bluff areas the top edge or crest of the bluff often is used. In low dune areas, the dune crest or edge of vegetation is used. The high tide line is used in many other jurisdictions. The hierarchy approach (see Chapter 6) used in administration of the Upton-Jones Amendment is effective in determining the proper reference feature for a national program.

Many state programs provide an additional setback over and above the average rate of recession, multiplied by the anticipated years of protection. The state of New York, for example, identifies the bluff face and crest as a special protective feature, allows no development on it, and measures the setback from the landward side of the feature. This has the effect of increasing the setback by 25 feet. In Michigan an additional 15 feet of setback is added to areas where recession rates vary in excess of a set formula. In North Carolina all erodible shores have a minimum setback of 60 feet, regardless of the rate of erosion.

Program Experience

States with an administrative experience in erosion setback programs believe their programs are important elements in property loss reduction. Although existing development continues to be threatened and lost, future development will be assured some minimum useful life. Almost all states have modified their original programs to improve effectiveness or correct unforeseen problems. Improvements such as having greater setback for large buildings, requiring movable building designs near the hazard area, establishing appropriate procedures to address additions or partially damaged structures, assessing the role of shore protection in setback regulations, and establishing procedures for updating or modifying setbacks have been addressed by several states.

State experience has shown that recession rate data must be updated periodically to reflect changes in the effectiveness of shore protection or beach nourishment; other human-induced changes such as dredging, harbor construction, and so on; water level fluctuations on the Great Lakes; subsidence or mean sea level rise; and other factors. Depending on the magnitude of change, updates may be required as infrequently as every decade or as frequently as after every major storm or hurricane. Pennsylvania and Indiana update their recession rate data using ground surveys conducted every 2 years. North Carolina updates using aerial photography every 5 years; Michigan and Texas update data every 10 years. Florida has updated its comprehensive survey for each county on an average of 10 to 12 years.

An erosion hazard management program will not realize its objectives without effective enforcement policies. These enforcement actions, which are time consuming, have been rare to date. Although state programs have had relatively few enforcement actions, failure to pursue aggressive enforcement results in reduced voluntary compliance.

States rarely have been challenged for a taking of property when imposing erosion setback regulations. This is believed to be because of several factors. First, the courts have a long history of upholding the public safety rationale of these kinds of regulations. Second, some programs will waive a portion of the setback if the property lacks sufficient depth. Third, many of the takings have been of privately owned property whose owners generally cannot afford the expense of a lawsuit against the state. Other programs allow a waiver for well-engineered shore protection and a maintenance plan. In addition, some people recognize that property that can no longer meet building requirements becomes substandard from natural erosion events as much as by regulation. Therefore, direct constitutional takings challenges have been rare.

Although state coastal zone erosion management programs are effectively addressing setbacks for new construction, they have had limited success in addressing losses in areas where development predates the implementation of the setback program. Nor have the states fully addressed the anticipated eventual losses to structures built following current setback guidelines—a structure with a useful life of 60 to 100 years eventually may be lost if built with a 30-year setback. States address this limitation in a variety of ways. Some states disseminate technical information on shore protection to encourage efforts to slow the historic rate of recession. Other educational efforts are designed to achieve a larger setback voluntarily. Some states require coastal structures to be placed on piling to prevent collapse during major storms. As a secondary benefit, these structures are readily moveable. Thus, the property owner clearly will have the option of relocation over shore protection or loss of the building in the future.

Even given the forethought many states have put into their erosion management programs, most states still face a series of dilemmas. First, if the state requires setbacks that are sufficient to protect new structures for the anticipated useful life of the structure (60 to 100 years), the setbacks may become too restrictive to obtain property owner or political support. In addition, existing structures are not addressed, including the need to demolish or relocate structures threatened from erosion loss. (A few states have provided low-interest loans or small grants to encourage relocation of houses threatened by erosion.) States generally lack the resources necessary to address the removal or relocation of threatened structures. In addition, a state with a more limited geographical scope is not as able to pool the risk as a federal program might be. Where shore protection is used to extend the life of buildings, problems associated with shore protection usually occur, including high cost, limited effectiveness, maintenance needs, adverse impacts on adjacent property, and loss of recreational beaches.

To provide specific examples of the nature of state coastal erosion management programs, this committee reviewed programs in four states: Michigan, North Carolina, Florida, and California.

MICHIGAN'S GREAT LAKES SHORELAND EROSION PROGRAM

At various times in Michigan's history, the hazards and costs of unwise development in erosion areas clearly have been demonstrated. In the early 1950s high water levels on the Great Lakes caused millions of dollars worth of damage to Michigan shoreline properties (Michigan Department of Natural Resources, 1982). During subsequent low water years, many homes were built too close to the bluffline. When high water levels returned in the late 1960s, damage to homes and businesses occurred once again. An estimated $46 million in property damage has been attributed to Great Lakes shore erosion occurring between Labor Day 1972 and Labor Day 1976. Another $50 million was spent on shore protection (University of Michigan, 1978). A preliminary survey for the period 1985 to 1987 showed the cost of high water levels in Michigan (both erosion and flooding) to be $222 million. A survey of the Lake Michigan shoreline of the Lower Peninsula of Michigan found 995 homes and cottages within 25 feet of the edge of active erosion. Erosion damage can be extremely costly both for property owners and the public. In past instances when severe storms have caused extensive erosion damage, the public has absorbed part of the loss through disaster assistance, disaster loans, and damage to public facilities. For example, after a 1973 storm, disaster declarations led to Small Business Administration loans and grants to property owners along southern Lake Huron for repair of shore protection and damaged homes. After a 1985 storm, the Michigan legislature appropriated $6 million to alleviate damage on public and private property.

The Shorelands Protection and Management Act, Public Act 245 of 1970, as amended, directs the Michigan Department of Natural Resources to (1) identify areas of high-risk erosion, (2) designate these areas and determine how they should be regulated to prevent property loss, and (3) enact administrative rules to regulate the future use and development of high-risk erosion areas (Shorelands Protection and Management Act, 1982). In addition, the Department of Natural Resources offers technical assistance to property owners and to local units of government to implement shorelands management activities.

The process by which Michigan carries out its management strategy for high-risk erosion areas includes the following:

1. *Identification of high-risk erosion areas.* High-risk erosion areas do not include all Great Lakes shorelines that experience erosion problems. Only those areas where the bluffline is receding (moving landward) at a long-term average of 1 foot or more per year are considered high risk. Of 3,288 miles of Great Lakes shoreline, Michigan has approximately 350 miles of shoreland that is classified as high-risk erosion areas.

2. *Designation of high-risk erosion areas.* To initiate formal designation of high-risk erosion areas, the department first seeks input from local units of government. Letters are sent to property owners who will be affected by the designation, notifying them that their property has been identified as a high-risk erosion area. The letter also invites property owners to a department-sponsored meeting where the program is explained and an opportunity for comment is provided. Those property owners who do not attend the meeting receive a second mailing that explains the proposed designation and its significance. After a period for comment, the department reviews all information and sends official letters to property owners whose

parcels are formally designated as high-risk erosion areas, and it notifies the appropriate local units of government of the designation.

3. *Implementation.* Michigan's program emphasizes a nonstructural approach to reduction of damages from shore erosion. This approach has been taken because structural protection in the form of erosion control devices may be prohibitively expensive in some cases, ineffective in others, and, if improperly designed, may accelerate erosion on adjacent property. The nonstructural program uses setback provisions to protect permanent structures from damage. In accordance with this approach, enlargements to existing structures and new permanent structures, including septic systems to be built in a designated high-risk erosion area, must be built a sufficient distance landward from the bluffline. Setback requirements achieve two main objectives. First, they alert the owner or buyer of shoreline property to the potential erosion hazard along a stretch of shoreline; second, the setback is designed to protect permanent structures for a period of 30 years. These regulations are implemented either through department-approved local zoning or state permit procedures.

Under Michigan's program, areas subject to serious shore erosion are identified initially by field survey. When evidence of active erosion is found, the area undergoes further study. Final classification of a high-risk erosion area is based on estimated long-term recession rate studies for the area.

Bluff recession is determined by comparing low-altitude aerial photographs of the shoreline from two different time periods and noting the change in position of the bluffline. Calculations then are made to determine the average annual recession rate. Two different photogrammetric methods are used. First, stereoscopic examination of photographs assists in accurate bluff detection. Second, the Zoom Transfer Scope is used to measure movement of the bluffline by superimposing the two photographic images. The average annual recession rate is determined for the last 20 to 50 years, a period during which both high and low water levels have occurred.

Bluffline setbacks are calculated from the average annual recession rate. The average annual recession rate is multiplied by 30 years. The resulting value then may be adjusted slightly for recession rate variability within an area. This process yields a distance, expressed in feet, that is the minimum required setback distance from the bluffline. Calculation of setbacks assumes that long-term recession rates will continue to be approximately the same in the future as they have been in the past.

The effect of the regulations on private property include the following:

1. *Building requirements.* Designation of a parcel as a high-risk erosion area affects the property owners if they wish to build a new permanent structure on the parcel or enlarge an existing structure. The building requirements call for any structure or enlargement to be set back from the bluffline by a minimum required distance that would protect the structure from erosion damage for about 30 years. Septic systems as well as buildings must adhere to the setback.

Some local units of government have adopted minimum setbacks in their zoning ordinances. Where setbacks have not been incorporated into zoning, the property owner must obtain a permit from the Department of Natural Resources before construction can begin. If the property lacks sufficient depth to meet the setback, a special exception may be granted.

2. *Special exceptions.* If a parcel established prior to high-risk erosion area designation lacks adequate depth to provide the minimum required setback from the bluffline, the parcel is termed a substandard lot. A special exception may be allowed on a substandard lot to permit the building of a structure as long as it can be moved before it is damaged by shore erosion. Special exceptions will be granted only as follows:

- A sanitary sewer is not used, and the septic system is located on the landward side of the movable structure.
- The movable structure is located as far landward as local zoning restrictions will allow.
- The movable structure is designed and built in accordance with proper engineering standards.
- Access to and from the structure site is of sufficient width and acceptable grade to allow for moving the structure.
- The foundation and other construction materials are removed and disposed of as part of the moving operation.
- If a substandard lot does not have access to and from the structure site of sufficient width and acceptable grade to allow for a movable structure, a special exception may be granted to utilize shore protection. The special exception will be granted only if the shore protection is designed to meet or exceed proper engineering standards for the Great Lakes and a professional engineer certifies that the shore protection has been designed and built in accordance with these standards.

If property owners appeal the high-risk designation or the disapproval of a permit, an administrative hearing is held. The proceedings of the hearing are forwarded to the Natural Resources Commission, which is composed of citizens appointed by the governor. The commission may reach a decision on the hearing officer's recommendations or it may hold additional hearings prior to reaching a decision. Should property owners disagree with the final decision and wish to carry the case further, they have 30 days after the commission's final determination to petition the Michigan Circuit Court for a judgment.

Michigan's Shorelands Protection and Management Act provides that local units of government may administer and enforce the minimum setback requirements established under the act by incorporating them into zoning ordinances. The primary advantage of local enforcement of shoreland regulations is that it increases the efficiency of administration. To ensure that shoreland ordinances meet the intent of the state legislation and comply with the minimum requirements for protection established by the state, ordinances and amendments must be reviewed and approved by the department. The department also periodically reviews the performance of local zoning authorities to ensure that administration is consistent with the legislation. In addition to zoning, local building code inspectors assist in the enforcement of shoreline setbacks through review of building permit applications. Building inspectors check each application in their jurisdiction to determine if the proposed construction is on a parcel of property designated as a high-risk erosion area. If it is, the building inspectors will withhold permits until they are assured that the state erosion setback permit has been issued.

NORTH CAROLINA'S COASTAL EROSION MANAGEMENT PROGRAM

North Carolina has 320 miles of ocean shoreline. Although 50 percent of this shoreline is in public ownership—primarily in two national seashores—the remaining half of the coastline faces substantial development pressure. No areas of the North Carolina coast contain the concentration of high-density development of Miami Beach, but few beach areas in the state retain the low-density, scattered cottage atmosphere associated with Nags Head in the 1940s.

Over the past 50 years, over half of the state's ocean coast has experienced average erosion rates of 2 feet per year or greater, with 20 percent exceeding 6 feet per year (Benton and McCullough, 1988).

Additional short-term fluctuations of the shoreline caused by storms also are common.

The management program that has evolved since 1974 in North Carolina has planning, regulatory, land acquisition, and policy development components (Owens, 1985). Two factors—increasing development and a dynamic shoreline—led the state over the past 10 years to develop a coordinated shore-front development program. The program regulates new development, restricts shore erosion-control practices, plans for redevelopment and relocation of damaged and threatened structures, purchases land for beach access, and develops public education programs. An exception to the erosion rate setback is allowed for lots that existed prior to 1979 and are not deep enough to meet the erosion setback. These lots must, however, meet the dune and 60-feet minimum setbacks.

The first step in the development of North Carolina's management program was setting clear goals. After considerable public debate about the physical, economic, and social factors affecting ocean-front development, the Coastal Resources Commission (the 15-member citizen policy-making body for the program) adopted three goals for the management program:

1. Minimize loss of life and property resulting from storms and long-term erosion.

2. Prevent encroachment of permanent structures on public beaches.

3. Reduce the public costs of inappropriately sited development.

North Carolina adopted a statewide minimum ocean-front setback for all new development in 1979. After several refinements in the early 1980s, the minimum setback now requires all new development to be located behind the farthest landward of these four points:

1. the erosion rate setback (30 times the annual erosion rate, measured from the vegetation line, for small structures; 60 times the erosion rate for structures with more than four units or more than 5,000 square feet total floor area);

2. the landward toe of the frontal dune;

3. the crest of the primary dune (the first dune with an elevation equal to the 100-year storm flood level plus 6 feet); or

4. a minimum of 60 feet (120 feet for larger structures), measured from the vegetation line.

Limited uses that do not involve permanent substantial structures (e.g., clay parking areas, tennis courts, and campgrounds) are allowed between the vegetation line and setback line, but no development is allowed seaward of the vegetation line.

Other regulatory provisions limit the intensity of development near inlets, set minimum construction standards, limit the construction of growth-inducing infrastructure in hazard areas, and restrict dune alteration.

Although these standards provide some degree of safety for new development, North Carolina has thousands of older structures increasingly threatened by coastal erosion and storms. Also, even new development eventually will face similar threats. Since the ocean beaches are a vital economic resource, the foundation of a tourism economy, and a key publicly owned recreational resource, the state has adopted a strong policy of protecting its beaches.

Effective January 1985, no erosion control devices designed to harden or stabilize the ocean beach's location are allowed in North Carolina. Bulkheads, seawalls, groins, jetties, and riprap are prohibited. Temporary sandbags are allowed, as is beach nourishment. An exception to the general prohibition is an emergency rule adopted in 1989 to allow the State Department of Transportation to construct a groin at the north end of Pea Island to provide protection to the foundations of the bridge across Oregon Inlet.

Effective in 1983, all coastal local governments in North Carolina have been required to include a hazard mitigation element in their mandatory land use plans. These plans include measures for prestorm mitigation, evacuation and recovery plans, and poststorm rebuilding policies. The latter are to give particular attention to the safe relocation of damaged roads, water and sewer lines, and other public investments.

Land acquisition also has been used as part of the state's oceanfront management efforts (Owens, 1983). The state's beach access program gives an explicit statutory priority to the acquisition of those lands that are unsuitable for permanent structures but that could be useful for beach access and use. Natural areas containing undeveloped beaches also have been acquired. A state income tax credit was adopted to encourage the donation of beach access and natural areas. Finally, public education has been a major priority, ranging from providing mandatory hazard notices and information to each permit applicant to broad community education on issues such as sea level rise, barrier island dynamics, dune and beach functions, and the like.

Coastal management in North Carolina during the past 15 years has demonstrated the necessity and effectiveness of state regional resource management. A successful coastal erosion management program must remain sensitive to local needs and desires for the future, incorporating the balance necessary to resolve equitably the conflicts between competing legitimate interests.

FLORIDA'S COASTAL EROSION MANAGEMENT PROGRAM

In 1968 the state of Florida initiated a comprehensive program of beach management. This program, in the Division of Beaches and Shores of the Department of Natural Resources, has grown from a single employee in 1968 to more than 75 employees in 1988. The program is broad and includes field measurements, research and analysis to determine causes of erosion, an extensive permitting and regulation program, and beach nourishment. The program encompasses 24 coastal counties, covering 648 miles of sandy beaches. To provide a better understanding of their beach resources, the state has installed a system of more than 3,400 concrete monuments at nominal spacings of 1,000 feet along 648 miles of sandy beach. Repeated profiles surveyed from these monuments have enabled accurate measurements of shoreline change over relatively short time spans (12 to 14 years). In addition, the state has funded the establishment of a comprehensive data base of shoreline positions using historic information. These shoreline positions are established at the locations of the monuments. For a typical county there may be five to six surveys spanning the time interval from the mid-1800s to the present. These data enable the computation of short- and long-term erosion rates. Three striking features of the erosion rates are (1) their high variability around the state, (2) the reasonably low magnitudes of the average erosion rate, and (3) the substantial effects of the channel entrances that have been established or modified for improved navigation.

A fundamental component of the Florida regulatory program is the Coastal Construction Control Line (CCCL), which establishes the state's jurisdiction in coastal construction permits. The line delineates the limit of "severe fluctuations" caused by a 100-year storm event and is based on an extensive investigative process including field surveys, aerial photography, and numerical modeling of storm surges and beach erosion. A state Department of Natural Resources permit is required for any excavation, construction, or alteration seaward of the line. Authorization for permit approval ranges from field inspectors for minor activities including dune walkover structures to the governor and cabinet (a seven-member body) for single-family dwellings and more extensive construction. Factors considered in permit approval include structure footprint, ability to withstand a 100-year storm event, proximity to the shoreline, erosion rate, shore-parallel coverage, and vegetation disturbance. State law also includes a 30-year erosion provision requiring, with minor exception, single-family dwellings to be set back 30 times the annual erosion rate. Multifamily dwellings are prohibited seaward of the 30-year erosion line. The 30-year erosion projections are referenced to the "seasonal high water line" contour. The seasonal high water elevation is referenced to National Geodetic Vertical Datum and is 1.5 times the mean tide range above mean high water. In contrast to the CCCL, which is set on a county-by-county basis, the 30-year erosion projection is established separately for each individual permit. State statutes relating to coastal construction are complemented by an explicit set of formal "rules."

Landward of the state coastal construction jurisdiction as established by the CCCL is the "Coastal Building Zone"—a zone under the jurisdiction of the various coastal counties designed to ensure the same integrity of coastal construction as that seaward of the CCCL. The Coastal Building Zone is defined to extend landward various distances depending on the coastal morphology. On barrier islands the Coastal Building Zone extends 5,000 feet landward from the CCCL or to the landward shoreline of the island, whichever is less. Along mainland shorelines, the Coastal Building Zone extends 1,500 feet landward from the CCCL.

State law also addresses the adverse effects that poor sand management practices at navigational channels have had on downdrift shorelines. Attempts are being made to reinstate the natural flow of sediments around these channels by installing and operating sand bypassing systems.

The Florida Department of Natural Resources proposed to the 1986 state legislature a 10-year, $472 million beach nourishment program for Florida's critically eroded beaches ($362 million for restoration and $110 million for renourishment). The initiative would cost an average of $2.6 million per mile to restore or renourish 140 miles of beaches; another $24 million would be needed annually for maintenance on an indefinite basis. The cost of nourishing beaches in five coastal regions would range from an estimated $1.9 million to $3.9 million per mile.

The recreation and economic benefits of beach restoration are intended to be realized by the entire state. Given the extent of current erosion conditions, Florida is proposing to share the cost of these projects on a fixed 75/25 percentage basis with local governments and private interests. This is a change from the traditional public/public financing of erosion control projects to a public/private partnership. For those projects with partial federal funding, the project costs would be decreased proportionally for the state, local, and private interests. Because this alternative is so costly, beach nourishment is most viable economically in areas with dense development, a large available sand supply, and relatively low wave energy. Few localities are fortunate enough to have all the characteristics to justify this approach as a long-range solution.

In Florida, where the benefits derived from the beaches are shared throughout the state, 67.3 miles of eroded beach has been restored or renourished from 1965 to 1984 at a total cost of $115 million ($1.9 million per mile for nourishment and $1.7 million per mile for renourishment) (State of Florida, 1986). Eighty-six percent of all funds expended were spent in the state's more heavily developed southeastern counties. Miami Beach alone has cost $5.2 million per mile to nourish 10.5 miles of beach front (Pilkey and Clayton, 1989). With the high cost of real estate (Miami Beach hotels recently were assessed at $235 million per mile) and the high tourist revenues, it is easy to generate a favorable benefit-cost ratio for coastal engineering projects.

CALIFORNIA'S COASTAL EROSION MANAGEMENT PROGRAM

California's coastal erosion problems are complex because of its pattern of coastal development, land morphology, and wave climate. Eighty percent of California's population of 26 million people live within 30 miles of the 1,100-mile shoreline (California State Senate, 1989). It extends in latitude from Boston, Massachusetts, to Charleston, South Carolina. While the task of developing a program to combat long-term coastal changes is a desirable policy objective, it has many policy and technical problems.

The land form of California is quite different from the Atlantic, Gulf, and Great Lakes coasts, leading to further differences in defining and dealing with coastal hazards. In California plate tectonics and the last excursion of sea level are key factors that have given rise to the series of coastal terraces that characterize most of California's coast. It is a "collision coast" (Inman and Nordstrom, 1971), and many sections of the coast are rising (Castle et al., 1976; Ewing et al., 1989). The other major feature of California's land form are drowned river valleys.

There are a number of state agencies concerned with various aspects of California's coastal zone management program. The major ones are the California Coastal Commission; California State Coastal Conservancy; Department of Boating and Waterways of the Resources Agency; State Lands Commission; Bureau of Land Management; Department of Parks and Recreation (the state park system includes 292 miles of ocean and bay frontage); State Water Resources Control Board, with its nine regional water quality boards; supra-agencies of local governments, such as the San Francisco Bay Conservation and Development Commission (BCDC, which has final authority over San Francisco Bay, rather than the Coastal Commission); San Diego Associations of Governments; and 70 coastal counties and cities. The Department of Boating and Waterways, among other things, is charged with coordinating the work of other state and local agencies and the U.S. Army Corps of Engineers in implementing the state's beach erosion-control program. The department also participates in the wave statistics gathering system, together with the U.S. Army Corps of Engineers, to gather nearshore and deep ocean wave data on a real-time basis, with the center located at the University of California at San Diego (Coastal Data Information Program, 1983). The department also funds studies to obtain other data and research in regard to sand sources by rivers, weather and climate variability along coastal southern California, currents off California's shore, and spatial structure of wind along the California coast.

The California Coastal Conservancy was created in 1976 by the state legislature to take positive steps to preserve, enhance, and restore coastal resources and to address issues that regulation alone cannot solve.

The California Coastal Commission, a regulatory agency, has had three stages: the original Coastal Zone Conservation Act of 1972; the first stage of the Coastal Act of 1976, which extended through the termination of the regional commissions in 1981; and the present stage, which began in 1981. These are summarized in

Table 5-2 (Fischer, 1985). Under the 1976 act, priorities for coastal usage are

- public access;
- public recreation;
- marine environments;
- land resources, including sensitive habitats and agricultural lands;
- development, with attention to concentration of new development, scenic resources, and development in hazard areas; and
- industrial development.

The act requires coastal localities to prepare their own plans for development within their jurisdiction—a Local Coastal Program (LCP). Many localities have broken up into smaller planning units, so it is anticipated that there will be a total of 126 LCPs. Until a region has an LCP certified by the Coastal Commission, all development permits must be requested from and issued by the commission. As of April 1989, 55 still do not have certified LCPs in place (California State Senate, 1989). In addition, the commission is to review each certified LCP every 5 years.

In addition to their regulatory and operational activities, each of these agencies issues reports, some of which are useful in coastal zone erosion management. One report, by the predecessor to the Department of Boating and Waterways, the Department of Navigation and Ocean Development, was referred to in Chapter 2 of this report (Habel and Armstrong, 1977). Another publication is "Coastal Protection Structures and Their Effectiveness" (Fulton-Bennett and Griggs, 1986). The California Coastal Conservancy has issued a number of reports, such as "Public Beaches: An Owners' Manual" (Mikkelsen and Neuwirth, 1987) and "The Urban Edge: Where the City Meets the Sea" (Petrillo and Grenell, 1985). The California Coastal Commission issues a large number of staff reports on specific cases that come before the commission. The commission also prepares more general technical reports, some specifically concerned with coastal erosion (Ewing et al., 1989; Howe, 1978). In making the commission the coordinator for the state's coastal policy and regulator of all coastal development (except within San Francisco Bay, for which the Bay Conservation and Development Commission [BCDC] is responsible), the act bestows on the commission the role

TABLE 5-2 Summary of the History of the Organization of the California Coastal Management Program

Implementation Phase	Organizational Structure	Definition of Coastal Zone	State Commission's Responsibilities	Relationship to Local Government
Coastal Zone Conservation Act of 1972, Proposition 20 (1973-1977)	Statewide commission, six regional commissions	Planning area: out to sea 3 miles, "inland to the highest elevation of the nearest coastal mountain range"; Permit area: 1,000 yards from mean high tide line	Regulate all development in permit area; prepare coastal plan for 1976 legislative session	Independent
Coastal Act of 1976 (1977-1981)	Same as 1973-1977	Out to sea 3 miles;[a] inland to boundaries set by state legislature[b]	Assist 52 cities and 15 counties in preparing local coastal programs; regulate development within entire coastal zone[c]	Close, collaborative

| Coastal Act of 1976 (1981-present) | One statewide commission | Same as 1977-1981 | As each local coastal program is certified, local government assumes authority to issue coastal permits consistent with its Local Coastal Program; commission takes secondary role of hearing appeals from local permit decisions, approving proposed amendments to Local Coastal Programs, providing technical assistance and advice, monitoring local permits to assure compliance, performing 5-year evaluations of Local Coastal Programs; commission retains original permit jurisdiction over state tidelands and performs all consistency reviews under federal Coastal Zone Management Act. | Advisory, appellate |

[a]For federal consistency purposes, activities in federal waters are reviewed if they have a "direct effect" on the coastal zone.
[b]The maps were posed on the walls of the Senate chamber in 1976, and each member suggested boundaries using flow pens; special-interest bills attempt to change the boundaries, usually unsuccessfully, each session.
[c]While the definition of "development" is the same as under Proposition 20, there are a number of categorical exclusions, such as repair/maintenance, minor expansions of existing structures, construction of new single-family houses in defined, and already urbanized neighborhoods, certain agricultural buildings, and the replacement of structures destroyed by natural disasters.

SOURCE: From Fischer, 1985.

of long-term planner for the coast's future. This requires in-depth research in areas such as the following:

• the consequences of the greenhouse effect and rising sea levels for the coast;
• the long-term prospects for and implications of offshore energy resource development;
• toxic and hazardous materials handling and spill cleanup in the coastal region;
• long-term land use possibilities and dangers for flood and geologic hazard areas;
• power plant development and siting;
• shore erosion, especially in developed areas; and
• scientific studies of existing coastal resources and the impact of planned development.

According to the California State Senate (1989) report, little of this has been done, owing largely to budgetary restraints. Some of the complexities encountered in a state as varied geographically and politically as California are discussed in the booklet "Coastal Recreation in California: Policy, Management, Access" (Heiman, 1986). The act mandates the creation of the Coastal Resource Information Center to collect information ranging from past Coastal Commission decisions to scientific studies and technical data relevant to specific portions of the coastal zone. Due largely to budgetary restraints, the center is not yet in operation (California State Senate, 1989).

There are several "wave climates," and the waves vary in intensity, number, and direction of approach. California's wave climate may be worsening, but there is no way to predict the future trend. The maximum waves of 1978 reshaped the statistical base of wave climates for California, increasing the size of the "100-year wave." The storms of the El Niño winter of 1982-1983 did it again for most of the state (Walker et al., 1984), and the storm of January 17-18, 1988, did it yet again for a section of southern California, with Seymour (1989) estimating it to have a recurrence interval of not less than 100-200 years. Second, it is clear after the integrated effects of the unprecedented series of storms in 1982 and 1983 and the January 17-18, 1988, storm that coastal erosion in California is not going to see all development in hazardous areas wiped out in one event. Rather, the pattern is one of damage and repair. Hazard abatement rather than redevelopment appears to be the logical response to that level of damage. It is the duration of the storm, the number of storms during the year, the direction from which waves approach the shore, the profile of sand or cobbles on the beach, and the configuration of the improvements that determine the degree of property damage.

The U.S. Army Corps of Engineers, Los Angeles District, has been making an intensive study ". . . to provide coastal data and information to planners and decisionmakers so that better and more informed decisions can be made regarding the restoration and maintenance of the 1,100 mile California coastline" (U.S. Army Corps of Engineers, 1983). Many reports were issued during 1987 and 1988, and the final reports are to be issued at the end of 1989. Most of the studies have been for southern California (see, e.g., U.S. Army Corps of Engineers, 1987 and 1988).

The storms of 1982 and 1983 caused over $100 million damage to structures and utilities located along the California coastline. Most of the structures damaged were constructed before the passage of the California Coastal Act of 1976. In order to minimize or prevent damage from storms such as those that battered the state in 1982 and 1983, the California Coastal Commission has attempted to regulate the design of structures in potentially hazardous areas. The Statewide Interpretive Coastal Act Guidelines contain a section that defines coastal bluff top areas that will require detailed geologic and/or engineering studies before a development permit can be issued by the commission.

Section 30253 of the Coastal Act states that "New development shall: (1) Minimize the risks to life and property in areas of high geologic, flood and fire hazard; (2) Assure stability and structural integrity, and neither create nor contribute significantly to erosion, geologic instability, or destruction of the site or surrounding area or in any way require the construction of protective devices that would substantially alter natural landforms along bluffs and cliffs."

As required by Coastal Commission guidelines, geotechnical studies are required within the "area of demonstration." The area of demonstration includes the base, face, and top of all bluffs and cliffs. The extent of the bluff top consideration should include that area between the face of the bluff and a line described on the bluff top by the intersection of a plane inclined at a 20 degree angle from the horizontal passing through the toe of the bluff or cliff, or 50 feet inland from the edge of the cliff or bluff, whichever is greater. In areas of known geologic stability or instability (as determined by adequate geologic evaluation and historic evidence), the commission may designate a lesser or greater area of demonstration.

All geotechnical reports for structures proposed to be located within the area of demonstration must consider, describe, and analyze the following:

1. cliff geometry and site topography;

2. historic, current, and foreseeable cliff erosion, including investigation of recorded land surveys and tax assessment records in addition to the use of historic maps and photographs, where available, and possible changes in shore configuration and sand transport;

3. geologic conditions, including soil, sediment, and rock types and structural features such as bedding attitudes, faults, and joints;

4. evidence of past or potential landslide conditions, the implications of such conditions for the proposed development, and the potential effects of the development on landslide activity;

5. impact of construction activity on the stability of the site and adjacent areas;

6. ground surface water conditions and variations, including hydrologic changes caused by the development (i.e., introduction of sewage effluent and irrigation water to the ground water system);

7. potential erodibility of the site and mitigating measures to be used to ensure minimized erosion problems during and after construction;

8. effects of marine erosion of sea cliffs;

9. potential effects of seismic forces resulting from a maximum probable earthquake; and

10. any other factors that might affect slope stability or littoral transport.

Because of the adverse impacts so commonly associated with large coastal protective devices (groins, breakwaters, etc.), the commission has favored the use of beach nourishment to reduce shoreline recession rates. However, it was decided that in some instances large coastal structures are the only viable alternative to solving a severe shore erosion problem. For example, in May of 1983 Chevron Oil Company applied for a permit before the commission to install a 900-foot-long semipermeable rock and concrete groin at the southern boundary of its waterfront refinery in El Segundo. As a result of the potential impacts, Coastal Commission permits typically have had conditions that attempt to satisfy the concerns of parties located immediately downdrift of the proposed structure. In the Chevron case, the following permit conditions were required by the commission and accepted by Chevron:

1. State Lands Commission approval;
2. utilization of aerial photographs to monitor project impacts;
3. beach profile readings at designated locations during specific times of the year;
4. sand tracer studies;
5. downdrift nourishment;
6. commitment to mitigate any adverse impacts to surfing conditions in the project vicinity;
7. a planned maintenance program;
8. a monitoring program to determine if fill material migrated back to the offshore site;
9. review of data by an unbiased third party;
10. an assumption of risk to indemnify and hold harmless the California Coastal Commission against any and all claims, demands, damages, costs, expenses, or liability arising out of acquisition, design, construction, operation, maintenance, existence, or failure of the permitted groin project; and
11. the above-mentioned conditions dealing with sand supply monitoring will exist for a period of 10 years.

SUMMARY

In the absence of a comprehensive program to address the nation's coastal erosion hazards, many states have implemented their own programs. The states' experience is valuable in the formulation of a national program. The committee considered this experience in formulating the recommendations for an effective and responsive minimum program (see Executive Summary). The Federal Emergency Management Agency should establish a program that supports accurate state, local, or university data acquisition efforts and encourages effective erosion area management at the state and local levels.

REFERENCES

Benton, S., and M. McCullough. 1988. Average Annual Long Term Erosion Rate Update Methods Report. Division of Coastal Management, Department of Natural Resources and Community Development, North Carolina.

California State Senate. 1989. Report on the California Coastal Commission, Advisory Commission on Cost Control in State Government. Submitted to the Senate Rules Committee pursuant to S.R. 40 (1984), April 1989, No. 409-S.

Castle, R. O., M. R. Elliot, J. P. Church, and S. H. Wood. 1976. The Evolution of the Southern California Uplift, 1955 Through 1976. U.S. Geological Survey Professional Paper 1342. Washington, D.C.: U.S. Government Printing Office.

Coastal Data Information Program. 1983. Monthly Reports, Institute of Marine Resources, Scripps Institution of Oceanography, University of California, San Diego, California.

Ewing, L. C., J. R. Michaels, and R. J. McCarthy. 1989. Draft Report: Planning for an Accelerated Sea Level Rise Along the California Coast. Staff Report, California Coastal Commission, June 26, 1989.

Fischer, M. L. 1985. California's Coastal Program. APA J. Summer:312-321.

Fulton-Bennett, K., and G. B. Griggs. July 1986. Coastal Protection Structures and Their Effectiveness. Joint publication of the California State Department of Boating and Waterways and the Marine Sciences Institute of the University of California at Santa Cruz.

Habel, J. S., and G. A. Armstrong. July 1977. Assessment and Atlas of Shoreline Erosion Along the California Coast. California Department of Navigation and Ocean Development. 277 pp.

Heiman, M. 1986. Coastal Recreation in California: Policy, Management, Access. Berkeley, Calif.: Institute of Governmental Studies, University of California.

Howe, S. 1978. Wave Damage Along the California Coast, Winter, 1977-78. Staff Report, California Coastal Commission, December 11.

Inman, D. L., and C. E. Nordstrom. 1971. On the tectonic and morphologic classification of coasts. J. Geol. 79:1-21.

Michigan Department of Natural Resources. 1982. Great Lakes Shorelands Erosion. Lansing, Mich.

Mikkelsen, T. H., and D. B. Neuwirth. 1987. Public Beaches: An Owners' Manual. Berkeley, Calif.: California State Coastal Conservancy in association with Western Heritage Press.

Owens, D. 1983. Land acquisition and coastal resources management: A programmatic perspective. William Mary L. Rev. 24:625.

Owens, D. 1985. Coastal management in North Carolina: Building a regional consensus. J. Am. Plan. Assoc. 51:322.

Petrillo, J., and P. Grenell, eds. 1985. The Urban Edge: Where the City Meets the Sea. Los Altos, Calif.: California State Coastal Conservancy in cooperation with William Kaufmann, Inc.

Pilkey, O. H., and T. D. Clayton. 1989. Summary of Beach Replenishment Experience on U.S. East Coast Barrier Islands. J. Coastal Research 5(1):147-159.

Seymour, R. J. 1989. Wave observations in the storm of January 17-18, 1988. Shore & Beach 57(4):10-13.

Shorelands Protection and Management Act. 1982. Lansing, Mich.: Michigan Department of Natural Resources.

State of Florida. 1986. A Proposed Comprehensive Beach Management Program for the State of Florida. Division of Beaches and Shores, Tallahassee, Florida.

University of Michigan Coastal Zone Laboratory. 1978. Michigan Shoreland Damage Assessment Program, 1977-1985, Technical Report No. 112.

U.S. Army Corps of Engineers. 1977. U.S. Great Lakes Shoreland Damage Study.

U.S. Army Corps of Engineers, Los Angeles District. 1983. Coast of California Storm and Tidal Waves Study: Plan of Study, September.

U.S. Army Corps of Engineers, Los Angeles District. 1987. Northern California Coastal Photography, Beach Profile and Bathymetry Index. Ref. No. CCSTWS 87-7.

U.S. Army Corps of Engineers, Los Angeles District. 1988. Coastal Cliff Sediments, San Diego Region to the Mexican Border (1887 to 1947). Ref. No. CCSTWS 88-8, December, prepared by Brian A. Robinson & Associates, Inc., Van Nuys, California.

Walker, J. R., R. A. Nathan, R. J. Seymour, and R. R. Strange III. 1984. Coastal Design Criteria in Southern California. Nineteenth Coastal Engineering Conference: Proceedings of the International Conference, September 3-7, 1984, Houston, Texas, ASCE, Vol. III, pp. 2827-2841.

6
Predicting Future
Shoreline Changes

INTRODUCTION

In order for the Federal Emergency Management Agency (FEMA) to administer the Upton-Jones Amendment, reliable erosion rate data for the U.S. coastlines are required. There are essentially two approaches for the acquisition of such data: analysis of historical shoreline changes to forecast future evolution and a statistical method (Monte Carlo simulations) based on synoptic oceanographic data (Table 6-1).

The first method is based on an analysis of the long-term data base of shoreline location, which must also take into account the time history of human interferences (e.g., beach nourishment, navigation entrances, dredging projects, sea walls, and groin emplacement). This analysis provides an average rate of evolution as well as a distribution of the fluctuations around the trend caused by seasonal variations and episodic storm events. The existing data base of shoreline locations generally is long term (many decades to over a century) and site specific.

The statistical approach is based on a knowledge of the deep and shallow water oceanographic environment (e.g., waves, wind current, storm surge) and sand sources and sinks that affect shoreline position. This information can be compiled as time series or statistical summaries. Sediment transport corresponding to a succession

TABLE 6-1 Methods for Determining the Rate of Shoreline Change

Methods	Shoreline Change Analysis	Monte Carlo Simulations
Data base	Shoreline data are site specific and discrete	Oceanographic data are synoptic and of coarse resolution
Phenomenological relationships	Not needed	Alongshore transport plus cross-shore transport combined
Calibration from shoreline change data	Interpretation only	Calibration of model for all categories of events
Advantages	Relatively simple	Physics-based approach
Disadvantages	Risk of bias on the effects of extreme events	Lack of accuracy of functional relationships
End product	Average yearly rate of erosion plus fluctuations around the average	Determination of probability distribution of shoreline locations with confidence bands
Implementation	Short term	Long term

of oceanographic events then is calculated based on physics-based equations relating the magnitude of forces causing the change to observed shoreline evolution.

The data base of deep-water oceanographic events is broad (i.e., valid for very large areas) and can be summarized statistically. Deep-water wave information for an ocean basin can theoretically be transformed into site-specific, shallow-water wave data that, in theory, can be used to determine long-term shoreline changes. The predicted shoreline fluctuations are then the result of the vagaries of the forcing functions (e.g., storm occurrence, El Niño conditions).

An additional consideration in evaluating these two approaches is the need of any insurance-based program to be able to assess the relative distribution of risks in order to establish appropriate insurance premiums. This task of establishing a commonality of risk is not easy, considering the following points:

1. A single common method of predicting shoreline changes, valid for all situations, does not appear to be possible, owing to

the extreme variations in coastal morphology and oceanographic climatology.

2. Risk is based on a combination of time-dependent effects from both long-term trend averages, which can be established from past observations of shoreline locations, and large fluctuations of stochastic processes, caused by the random nature of storms. On an eroding beach of established evolution, the average risk increases with time. Seasonal fluctuations (winter-summer profiles in some regions) can be added (based on previous field data) to long-term profile change. However, damage often occurs during an unpredictable short-term episodic event or perturbation that takes place in addition to (and contributes to) general shore erosion.

This chapter reviews the validity and limitations of the two major approaches for predicting future shoreline changes. The recommended approach for FEMA in determining shoreline change is the "Monte Carlo" method, but its utility presently is limited by the lack of sufficient correlated oceanographic and shoreline change data. Therefore, an interim methodology (historical shoreline analysis), which is based on good-quality shoreline change data and an appropriate computer-based processing system, should be implemented. It is proposed that this interim methodology should be improved by incorporating existing data on oceanographic forces with correlated observations of shoreline change.

HISTORICAL SHORELINE CHANGE METHOD

Available Data Base

A wide variety of data and information on beach erosion exist for the Atlantic, Gulf of Mexico, Pacific, and Great Lakes coasts. The information, however, ranges from highly accurate engineering surveys to fairly general comparisons of historical photographs and maps at various scales. The primary federal agencies engaged in the systematic collection of coastal information are the U.S. Army Corps of Engineers (COE), the National Oceanic and Atmospheric Administration (NOAA), and the U.S. Geological Survey (USGS). In 1971 the COE published an inventory of the nation's coastlines in "A Report on the National Shoreline Study." Unfortunately, the report was broad and had limited usefulness, but it is the only comprehensive, nationwide assessment of America's coasts.

Additional information is available from the 30 coastal states as well as local governmental departments, colleges, and universities carrying out coastal research and from private engineering and environmental consulting firms. For example, New Jersey, Delaware, North Carolina, Florida, Louisiana, California, Michigan, and Illinois all have active coastal data collection programs for management purposes.

Changes in shore position have been delineated using a wide range of methodologies, including field measurements of beach profiles (e.g., Dewall and Richter, 1977), visual comparison of historic changes from hand-held photography (Johnson, 1961; Kuhn and Shepard, 1980), and quantitative analysis of historical maps and vertical aerial photography through various photogrammetric procedures (Leatherman, 1983a). Although field measurements have the potential to yield the most accurate data to determine beach changes, the utility of such information is severely constrained because of its temporal and spatial nonhomogeneity. Florida has the best statewide program for the collection of such information, where 10 to 15 years of data are available. For the other coastal states, such data are not even available for most beaches, and the record often extends for a decade or less for even the best-monitored recreational beaches.

The data needed for shoreline mapping can be obtained from maps and charts and aerial photographs. Within NOAA the National Ocean Service (NOS) performs coastal surveys of the United States and its territories. For many coastal areas NOS topographic surveys are available dating from the mid-1800s. When historical data are compared to modern high-quality maps, long-term rates of coastal erosion and accretion can be computed. These maps can be augmented and updated with historical aerial photographs (late 1930s to present) available from many public agencies; the USGS's National Cartographic Information Center (NCIC) serves as a central repository of such data. The NOS "T" (topographic) sheets are generally the most accurate maps available for the coastal zone. Stable points located on these maps are accurate to within 0.3 mm of their actual positions at the scale of the map (often 1:10,000). The smallest field distance measurable is between 7 and 16 feet. This high accuracy makes them quite useful in delineating the land-water boundary and particularly for determining net changes over the long term. Along the Great Lakes, seasonal and long-term changes in water levels make the bluff top edge a better measure of erosional trends than the wetted bound.

The USGS topographic maps can provide additional detail in comparison to NOS T sheets, but these maps are updated at infrequent intervals. Also, their accuracy is a problem since the USGS topographic maps are produced just within the guidelines of National Map Accuracy Standards, which allows for no more than 10 percent of the stable points tested to be in error by more than one-fiftieth of an inch at the scale of the map. On the standard 7.5-minute quadrangles (1:24,000), one-fiftieth of an inch would mean an error of 40 feet in the actual location of a stable point. Other points, such as shoreline positions, are located with an even larger potential error.

Aerial photographs can be used to provide the necessary detail and short-time interval required to detect and evaluate the processes shaping the coastline. The use of vertical air photographs to determine the rates of shoreline change at selected points was well documented by Stafford (1971). Since then a number of coastal scientists have used air photos to monitor shoreline recession (Dolan et al., 1978; Leatherman, 1979) and to quantify changes in barrier environments (Leatherman and Zaremba, 1986). It must be remembered that air photos are not maps, and corrections for a range of distortions must be made to rectify this imagery for usage in quantitative analysis.

In most cases final maps are produced by transferring the air photo data to an appropriate base map, and the readily available USGS topographic maps often have been selected for this purpose. As previously discussed, these maps have a 40-foot potential error to which any errors associated with air photo mapping would be added. The product is a map of relatively low accuracy, and only major changes in the shoreline can be measured meaningfully.

Shoreline Indicator for Mapping Purposes

The shoreline is defined as the interface between the land and water. However, the position of the shoreline on the beach face is highly variable because of changes in water level caused by tides, waves, and wind and on the Great Lakes by hydrologic factors.

The mean high water line is depicted on NOS T sheets as the shoreline indicator. It is preferred to any other tidal boundary for the shoreline indicator because this wetted bound can be recognized in the field and approximated from air photos. This allows for the direct comparison of data obtained from the NOS T sheets and vertical aerial photographs. While vegetation lines are easily recognized on photographs, such information was not always recorded on the historic NOS T sheets. Because the T sheets are referenced to mean high water (MHW) and this is virtually the only long-term data on historical shoreline changes available, this shoreline indicator has been adopted by most coastal investigators for mapping purposes. It should be kept in mind that the longer the period of record, the greater confidence and reliability can be placed on the trend measurement of shoreline change, provided there are a sufficient number of data sets.

Error Analysis of Map Compilation

Beach erosion measurements are subject to a variety of error sources, depending on the exact methodology used in the historical shoreline change analysis. A discussion and comparison of the various mapping procedures appear elsewhere (Leatherman, 1983a). A conservative (worst-case) estimate of the maximum possible error in high-quality techniques of analyzing historical shoreline data approaches 40 feet, which is within National Map Accuracy Standards. In practice, errors often have been shown to be less than 20 feet, the average being 11 feet for the Delaware coastal erosion mapping project (Galgano and Leatherman, 1989).

Projection of Shoreline Positions

Extrapolation of trends based on historical shoreline change analysis takes into consideration the inherent variability in shoreline response based on differing coastal processes, sedimentary environments, and coastal exposures. The following discussion concerns the validity of determining long-term shoreline position changes from limited observations (e.g., snapshot views of the beach through time via time-series air photos).

For the sake of simplicity, consider a hypothetical case where the shoreline location is defined as a function of time. The trends in shoreline position shown on the two curves (Figure 6-1) correspond to differences in the length of record available. The average rate of shoreline position change with respect to time is different for the record extending from 1920 to 1930 as compared to the 1920 to 1940 record. This difference is caused by the occurrence of extreme events in 1927-1930, for example, a hurricane in 1930 and the fact that accretion took place between 1930 and 1937.

The important point to consider in this hypothetical illustration (Figure 6-1) is that the estimation of shoreline trend depends on both the long-term trend ("signal") and short-term "noise" caused by seasonal and storm (hurricane-induced) effects. To quantify this point, suppose the shoreline position trend rate is 1 foot per year and the noise range is 100 feet (an extreme example). If it is desired to limit the error in defining the trend to ±30 percent, the required time period of measurement to meet these conditions is 333 years. As a comparison, suppose the shoreline position trend rate is 20 feet per year, with the noise range and error limit the same. In this case the required time period of measurement is only 16.7 years. The significance of these two examples is that if it is necessary to establish, with confidence, the shoreline change trend in locations where the trend is small to moderate, the required time periods of measurement can be longer than the data record available. Realizing that a portion of the noise at a point is time dependent—for example, caused by seasonal and storm effects—and a portion is caused by spatial (alongshore) effects, it is possible to decrease the necessary measurement time interval by averaging the shoreline changes alongshore. In addition, poststorm and wintertime photos should not be compared to imagery acquired in the summer.

Rates of beach recession can be calculated from the change in shoreline or bluff position over time. If a number of historic shoreline positions are available, then it is possible to determine rates of change in beach recession both temporally and spatially. Of course, this straightforward projection of new shoreline position based on historical change assumes that all the oceanographic forces (e.g., waves and sea level change) remain essentially constant. If the greenhouse-induced climate warming increases, then the rate of sea level rise likely will accelerate in the future, so adjustments must be made to project further sea level rise/shoreline movement relationships (Leatherman, 1983b).

In summary, erosional trend rates can only be established accurately in those areas where long-term shoreline positions are available or where the trend rates are large. Where beach erosion rates are calculated to be in the low range (1 foot or less per year), it must be realized that the reliability of this measurement is probably low owing to natural fluctuations in beach width. Therefore, prudence demands that a certain minimum setback distance be added to the average annual erosion rate to compensate for the larger possible error in trend measurements.

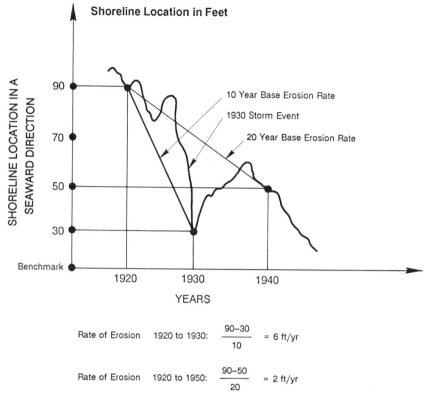

FIGURE 6-1   Example of the variation of the rate of erosion as a function of the duration of the period of observation, 1920 to 1940.

Existing Nationwide Data on Beach Erosion

Maps depicting shoreline changes along portions of the U.S. coasts have been made for a host of reasons and by literally hundreds of researchers using a range of methodologies. For instance, the New Jersey coast has been mapped to determine beach erosion rates by at least three separate groups during the past few decades (Dolan et al., 1978; Farrell and Leatherman, 1989; Nordstrom, 1977). In addition to these statewide mapping efforts, other agencies (e.g., U.S. Army COE) have mapped specific portions of the New Jersey coast. Mapping methodologies have ranged from photocopy reduction/enlargement of historical maps and photos for direct overlay to sophisticated computer-based mapping methodologies that permit correction of the inherent errors and distortions of the raw data.

The USGS has compiled these widely disparate historical data on erosion rates as part of the *National Atlas* series (Dolan et al., 1985). The *National Atlas* is plotted at a scale of 1:6,000,000, and recession rates are displayed at intervals of 1 meter per year of shore change. Although this map provides an overview of the national coastal recession situation, it has limited utility because of its coarse resolution.

The data used for the USGS *National Atlas* on shore change exist at a better resolution for most locations and are on an IBM-compatible PC. This system, called the Coastal Erosion Information System (CEIS), also contains a bibliography of reference sources and is capable of computing standard statistical parameters (erosion rates, standard deviation, and running means) at selected distances along the shoreline.

The CEIS approach has limited utility for FEMA because there is essentially no quality assessment of the input data. Further limitations exist because most of the data records are temporally short (decades) and a variety of mapping methodologies have been used to produce the data, which therefore vary widely in resolution and reliability. The CEIS data assembly does provide a general qualitative index of erosion-prone areas along U.S. coasts, but the data are not sufficient to help implement an interim methodology for FEMA.

An example of the implementation of the historic shoreline change method is illustrated by the New Jersey coastal erosion project. The raw data used included all available NOS T sheets, New Jersey Department of Environmental Protection orthophotos, and a specially acquired set of large-scale vertical aerial photographs for the Atlantic coast beaches. Five sets of T sheets were available from the NOS archives, ranging in age from the mid-1800s to the 1960s. The state orthophotos (based on air photos corrected for distortion by stereoplotters) were of 1970s vintage. A professional aerial survey company was commissioned to fly the coast to obtain the most recent data on shoreline position. Engineering surveys of particular areas were available for many towns but were not used because of their limited coverage on a statewide basis. Also, the USGS T maps (7.5-minute quadrangles) were not used because the historical shoreline change maps and hence calculation of beach erosion rates would have been considerably less accurate.

The Metric Mapping computerized technique of data entry, distortion correction, and map plotting was used to generate the historical shoreline change information (Leatherman and Clow, 1983).

Approximately eight shorelines covering a period of the past 130 years now are available to determine the long-term trend in beach erosion. Only good, high-quality raw data were used; the orthophotos and air photos acquired during summertime for seasonal consistency were selected to complement and update the NOS T sheets. Other aerial photographic data were available, but the number of sets used was limited by the funds available. The total cost for erosion mapping was approximately $2,000 per mile of shoreline. New Jersey's data requirements for the continued implementation of its building setback regulations are for an erosion update every 5 to 10 years.

PREDICTIVE MODELS

Background

Within the past several decades there has been substantial interest in the development of calculation procedures (herein termed "models") for quantitative prediction of future shoreline changes as a result of natural or human-induced effects. These models, which include both analytical and numerical types, are well beyond the infancy stage and provide a sound foundation for the recommended longer-term methodology, yet they are not presently at a level where they can be applied and interpreted without substantial effort and skill. Therefore, these models cannot be applied easily in their present form to the type of predictions needed to implement a FEMA erosion program.

The paragraphs below provide a brief overview of the status of modeling of beach systems. Appendix C presents a more detailed review, including a discussion of the features of individual models.

Shoreline retreat can occur as a result of longshore sediment transport, offshore sediment transport, or a combination. Offshore sediment transport primarily is responsible for shoreline retreat during storms, whereas long-term retreat can be caused by either or by a combination of these transport components. Individual models have tended to concentrate on shore response to either longshore or cross-shore transport. Models are generally site specific for erosion and require validation against the history of a particular site.

A process-based model requires two types of equations: (1) a transport equation relating the volumetric movement of sediment to the causative forces (e.g., waves, tides, etc.), and (2) an equation that carries out the bookkeeping of changes as a result of the sediment movement. Some of the earliest modeling efforts simplified the above equations for the case of longshore sediment transport, thus allowing analytical solutions to be developed that provide considerable insight into the effects of individual parameters, such as wave height and direction. Larson et al. (1987) have summarized a number of such solutions, including the effect of constructing a groin along the shoreline, evolution of a beach nourishment project, and shoreline changes from delivery of sediment to the coast by a river. In addition to analytical solutions, numerical solutions have been developed that allow specification of time-varying waves and tides.

Cross-shore transport models have received little attention until the last few decades. These models generally are based on the concept that if the prevailing waves and tides are of sufficient duration the profile will evolve to an equilibrium shape. The complexity of these models ranges from simple ones based on correlation with field and laboratory data to those that simulate profile evolution based on time-varying wave heights and storm surges as input. The state of Florida uses a simplified version of a cross-shore model in defining the zone of impact owing to a 100-year storm event.

Within the last decade models have been extended to represent both longshore and cross-shore transport. This capability is especially important in situations involving structures where the interruption of longshore transport (e.g., by a groin) causes increases and decreases in the profile slope on the updrift and downdrift sides of the structure and corresponding cross-shore transport components.

At present, longshore transport models probably are accurate to within ± 30 percent and cross-shore transport models to within ± 60 percent, providing there is no storm-induced interruption to the assumed prevailing condition. They are, however, the type of operational tool that would be highly useful eventually to a FEMA erosion program.

Perlin and Dean (1985) have developed an n-line model in which both longshore sediment transport and cross-shore sediment transport are represented. As an example of its application, consider transport in the vicinity of one or more groins. Updrift and downdrift of a groin, the shoreline would be displaced seaward and landward, causing an increase and decrease in the profile slopes, respectively, and thereby inducing offshore and onshore components, respectively, of cross-shore sediment transport. At each time step, the governing equation is solved by matrix inversion.

Limitation of Existing Modeling Methodology

Both episodic (storm) events and long-term prevailing wave climatology influence the alongshore and cross-shore transport of sediments and, consequently, the resulting displacement of the shoreline. If one considers the cross-shore transport alone, then generally the relative balance between waves (and storm surge) causing erosion and swell waves causing accretion determines the long-term evolution of the shoreline. On many shorelines the seasonal changes in sea and swell cause cross-shore erosion/accretion fluctuations of the shoreline.

Theoretically, given functional relationships relating the oceanographic wave conditions to longshore and cross-shore transport, predictive methodology can be devised through mathematical modeling and statistics. However, even though much progress has been made in the understanding of surf zone hydrodynamics, there remain a number of gaps, particularly relating the hydrodynamics functionally to the distribution of sediment transport. Furthermore, these processes are highly nonlinear; therefore, cumulative effects of longshore and cross-shore transports cannot be obtained deterministically from a wave rose such as found in climatological atlases (Le Mehaute et al., 1981 and 1983). Even if one considers a single mode of transport, either longshore or cross-shore, the effects of a time series of wave forcing on shoreline dynamics cannot be added linearly.

Because of this nonlinearity, the results over a number of climatologic events vary with the sequential order of the wave events (i.e., the same wave climatology does not necessarily yield the same shoreline evolution but depends upon the order of events). For example, 1 month of prevailing waves followed by a 2-day storm does not yield the same results as a 2-day storm followed by 1 month of prevailing waves, everything else being equal. Finally, littoral transport is a nonlinear, sensitive function of wave approach direction, and wave rises are reported too coarsely for an accurate determination of littoral drift.

Given reliable functional relationships between wave-surge-current and sediment transport, only short-term episodic events can in theory be analyzed deterministically based on the short time history of the incident waves and surge during these individual storms. Under these conditions, short-term evolution of shorelines can be predicted deterministically in the two cases where (1) shoreline changes are the result of variations of longshore drift because of wave refraction and curvature of the bottom contours (Le Mehaute and Soldate,

1980; Perlin and Dean, 1986) and (2) shoreline change is the result of cross-shore movement from waves and storm surge combined (Kriebel and Dean, 1985). This is described in Appendix C of this report. However, it is reemphasized that these two methods are based on functional relationships that must be improved by further research.

A COMPREHENSIVE METHOD OF PREDICTING SHORELINE CHANGES

Background

Shoreline displacement is influenced both by the long-term prevailing wave climate of frequent occurrence (i.e., of high probability) and by rare, extreme episodic events of low probability. It is influenced also by the quantity and quality of sand sources and sinks and by human-induced factors.

Wave climate summaries provide a large population of oceanographic events over a relatively short period of time (years to decades). The sequential time history of these numerous events is seldom available. Most likely they are grouped statistically in the form of probability of exceedance curves and wave roses. Because these data are based on a large population, they generally are reliable. However, because of cumulative errors over a large number of events (and their sequential and nonlinear effects), shoreline changes cannot be determined by the phenomenological deterministic approach at this time. Their average effects can be obtained theoretically from the site-specific data base of shoreline change over a relatively short period of time, *excluding* the effect of extreme events. Unfortunately, adequate data for this purpose are seldom available.

Episodic storms present a relatively smaller population of events, requiring a much longer period of observation than may be available from the site-specific and duration-limited shoreline data base. However, a data base of the causative oceanographic events valid for a broad area over generally longer periods of time may be available, from which site-specific forcing events can be determined. Then, formulation of the functional relationships relating sediment transport to these forcing events can allow for determination of shoreline changes. These functional relationships can be calibrated from the site-specific shoreline data under extreme conditions and the post-storm recovery time. Then, by adding their effects linearly, the cumulative shoreline changes from a series of extreme events of known probability can be calculated deterministically. For example, this approach can cover a distribution of extreme events occurring over a century. The data base can be extended synthetically and the method can be refined by application of a method currently in use by FEMA to establish storm surge statistics.

Method Based on Monte Carlo Simulations

The method described in the preceding paragraphs requires that it be valid to add linearly the effects of all oceanographic events. Actually, beach changes are caused by every uncorrelated event, depending upon the initial conditions resulting from the previous change. In particular, beach accretion following a storm (i.e., during recovery time) depends upon the plan and profile, the topography and bathymetry left by the storm, and the movement of nearby estuaries, etc. Owing to the lack of a complete time history of sea state and the sequence dependence and nonlinear nature of the related beach processes, a stochastic approach to shoreline evolution is necessary for scientific exactness. The problem is indeed inherently chaotic (i.e., deterministic but unpredictable). A Monte Carlo simulation of incident waves provides a method consistent with the natural processes. This method translates the random nature of the sea state into deterministic events, the sum of which gives the same wave energy rose as provided by summary atlases. Shoreline evolution then is determined statistically by a succession of Monte Carlo simulations of wave climatology, including both prevailing wave conditions and storms (Le Mehaute et al., 1983). The forcing functions are randomly defined by season and by a multiplicity of time series of varying events (e.g., direction, intensity, etc.) that can all be grouped in the same statistical summaries.

The random nature of oceanographic events is accounted for by a large number of Monte Carlo simulations for the same location. The Monte Carlo simulations of wave approach direction at fine resolution, in addition to the multiplicity of wave energy levels, also alleviates the discrepancy resulting from the coarse discretization of the wave angle from the atlases. Multiple Monte Carlo simulations for the same location allow the determination of a multiplicity of shoreline distances from a reference point, from which a probability distribution of shoreline locations can be obtained as a function of time. Standard deviation and confidence bands that increase with time and number of simulations also can be obtained.

The Monte Carlo simulation also could be used for determining storm surge statistics as well as the Joint Probability Method presently used by FEMA. The Monte Carlo simulation has not been used due to the relative complexity of storm surge calculations and the large number of simulations that this method requires. (Typically, 300 storm surge calculations for each study area are needed for the Joint Probability Method.) However, the Monte Carlo simulation for storm surge is not needed, since storm surges are independent events and their effect on flooding generally is not cumulative.

Even though it represents a physically more complex phenomenon than storm surges, the mathematical modeling of shoreline evolution is relatively straightforward. This allows the processing of a great number of simulations as required by the Monte Carlo method. In principle, the Monte Carlo simulations provide as many shoreline positions as needed for determining confidence bands and standard deviations. The most significant limitation of Monte Carlo simulation is our present poor understanding of beach recovery time scales that would be required to provide an initial condition for each succeeding event to be modeled.

Even in the case of well-documented, long-term statistics of prevailing climatology and episodic events, the state of the art is such that this approach, even though desirable, is difficult at this time. This is due primarily to the lack of reliable functional relationships relating the physics of sediment transport to the forcing events. In particular, more research and understanding are needed of the processes relating to the long-term erosion trend and the recovery of beaches following storms. Nevertheless, because it is practically the only theoretically rational approach to the problem, every effort should be made for its development and application. A summary and comparison of the Historical Shoreline Analysis and Monte Carlo simulation methods are presented in Table 6-1.

FEMA's Present Methodology

DEFINITION OF IMMINENT COLLAPSE

A house is defined as in danger of imminent collapse (1) if its distance from shore is less than a critical distance defined below and (2) if its structural integrity and, in particular, its foundation do not satisfy construction code criteria such as described in the FEMA report (January 22, 1988) on "structure subject to imminent collapse." The reference line from which the requisite distance is to be measured is defined as follows:

1. bluff edge;
2. top edge of escarpment on an eroding dune (normal high tide should be near the toe of the dune and there should be indications that the dune is actively eroding);
3. normal high tide line, which is indicated by the following:
   a. vegetation line (must be in an area of low tidal range where permanent vegetation exists just above high tide),
   b. beach scarp (a 4- to 10-inch cut at the upper limit of high tide),
   c. debris line (deposited by the normal high tide), and
   d. upper limit of wet sand; and
4. vegetation line (when none of the above can be located, use the seaward-most edge of permanent vegetation—this is intended to be seldom used).

This list is presented in priority order; if the first recommended feature is not present or suitable for use, the next feature should be used, and so forth. However, only the first two reference features are appropriate for use with the interim methodology recommended herein.

In most state programs the setback line refers to a fixed baseline determined at a given time and rarely changed. In the present context the reference line is continuously moving shoreward and must be reviewed annually at the time of the construction permit process. Accordingly, the reference line may vary for two adjacent structures built at two different periods of time.

The distance from that line defining the zone of imminent collapse is obtained by the sum of five times the annual rate of erosion and an additional distance defined by a 50 percent probability that the distance will be exceeded within the next 3 years. For lack of accurate determination of the confidence bands allowing an accurate definition of the 50 percent probability deviation from the mean, a 10-foot distance will be added to the five times annual rate of erosion.

RECOMMENDED METHODOLOGIES

Introduction

The following two methodologies are recommended by the committee for use in determining shoreline change rates. The committee recognizes that the use of available shoreline recession data such as aerial photos and profiles would be the least costly to implement shoreline change mapping. However, it would be preferable, although more costly, to utilize oceanographic data in the determination of shoreline change rates.

Historical Shoreline Change Method

Historical shoreline mapping can immediately provide the requisite data on erosional trends for implementation of the FEMA program. While there is already a plethora of such data available for the U.S. coasts, standards must be set and met for inclusion of such information into the national computerized data bank.

There are three basic requirements for the acquisition of reliable, accurate, and readily usable information on erosion rates as determined from historical shoreline analysis:

1. Use of only good-quality raw data (from high-quality maps, large-scale air photographs, and survey profiles).

2. Utilization of a mapping procedure that allows for the compilation of both map and air photo data and that permits the rectification of these raw data such that they meet or exceed National Map Accuracy Standards.

3. Output of PC-based digital data in the State Plane Coordinate System that readily permits the calculation of erosion rates at a predetermined basis along the shoreline or at specified locations and includes a map-plotting capability on a PC-based system.

Determination of the erosion trend should be based on the longest period of record available, but provisions must be made for any human-induced effects (e.g., groins, jetties) on shoreline position during recent times. The earliest reliable maps commonly available for the U.S. coasts are the NOS T sheets. There are approximately 6,000 T sheets available from NOS archives in Rockville, Maryland. The earliest information dates from the mid-1800s and extends to the 1970s; for many coastal areas, approximately four sets of historical maps are available at 30-year intervals. All rectifiable NOS T sheets should be utilized in a long-term analysis of historical shoreline changes.

Vertical aerial photography should be used to complement and update the NOS map data. Literally millions of historical air photos exist of the U.S. coasts. The earliest imagery dates from the late 1930s and early 1940s to the present. From the 1960s to date, most coasts have been photographed at 5-year intervals by various agencies (e.g., USDA, SCS, COE, DOI). Urbanized coasts, such as Ocean City, Maryland, are now photographed several times a year by professional aerial survey companies. Therefore, lack of data generally is not a problem, and its selection for mapping typically is governed by the coverage and scale.

Good-quality raw maps and air photo data still must be corrected for distortion or otherwise rectified to make them usable for the determination of reliable, accurate rates of beach or bluff erosion. A host of methodologies have been utilized in the past, ranging from photocopy reduction/enlargement of air photos and maps for direct overlay comparisons to sophisticated computer-based mapping systems (Leatherman, 1983a). It must be clearly understood that the best raw data cannot be expected to yield high-quality erosion rate information without proper corrections/rectifications to remove inherent errors and distortions. The compiled data on historical shoreline changes should in any case meet or exceed National Map Accuracy Standards.

Shoreline change maps and the derived rates of beach erosion must be interpreted by professionals; otherwise, misleading or even wrong conclusions can be drawn from a causal inspection of the data. For example, a variety of patterns of shoreline behavior (e.g., linear recession, cyclic changes near inlets, and engineering structural-induced trends) exhibited along the New Jersey coast are determined from the historical data (Farrell and Leatherman, 1989). Therefore, professional judgment is required for proper interpretation and application of erosion data for the FEMA program.

There are two possible outputs for the erosion data: tabular format or map products. Both products are desirable as each has special advantages to FEMA in terms of information display and analytic calculations. The historical shoreline change data should be in digital format on a State Plane Coordinate System for computational ease. A PC-based, user-friendly, menu-driven system should be utilized to facilitate calculation of erosion rates on a predetermined basis (e.g., 50 meters) along the shoreline or at specified locations of particular interest. In addition, FEMA personnel should have the option of viewing the data in map format, wherein all or a specified portion of the historical shorelines appear in their spatial context. Oftentimes, this spatial representation of the shoreline data can be invaluable in understanding apparent anomalies in the beach erosion data as it appears in tabular form.

Long-Term Methodology

In a previous section the recommended E-10, E-30, and E-60 zones are defined by the distance between the reference line and 10 times, 30 times, or 60 times the annual rate of erosion, respectively. This is based on the assumption that the erosion rate is constant over time and is determined by the historical shoreline change method.

In actuality, erosion rates can vary through time, depending upon the geological features of the substrata. For example, a rock formation may be uncovered by erosion, which would not respond to waves as readily as loose sand. Conversely, dune overtopping and massive overwashing could increase the amount of storm-induced beach erosion.

The long-term methodology provides a better definition of the E-zones by taking into account the probability distribution of shoreline location from short-term climate variation (such as storms) about a slowly changing average location. Once this long-term methodology is implemented, a redefinition of the E-zones is recommended, commensurate with the new knowledge obtained.

Beach erosion trends can be determined by the historical shoreline mapping methodology until this preferred long-term approach of using oceanographic data and statistical treatments can be undertaken. In actuality, the preferred methodology involves utilizing available records of shoreline recession for analysis of the time history of oceanographic forces (e.g., wind waves, storm surges, etc.). For lack of data, established functional relationships (relating longshore transport to the incident alongshore wave energy on the one hand and cross-shore transport to the onshore wave energy and storm surge on the other hand) will be used, as described in a previous section.

Following the availability of long-term oceanographic data, statistical methods can be introduced to improve the accuracy of shore prediction. Standard variation and confidence bands about the average or most probable shoreline location also can be defined. As previously stated, implementation has to remain flexible, considering the geographic variability of coasts, because a set relationship valid at one place may not be valid elsewhere.

Time and availability of resources are also a factor in implementation of a statistical approach. Initially, a ranking based on storm intensity may be used, but results from Monte Carlo simulations are much desired. The corresponding methodologies should be developed in parallel in order to assess the errors and discrepancies between various approaches by sensitivity analysis.

It is anticipated that this program will be implemented county by county. At a later date, the matching of the prediction at the boundaries of each county will be required so as to make the result consistent for sake of fairness in the insurance rate.

ESTABLISHMENT OF A COMPUTERIZED NATIONAL DATA BASE

A tremendous amount of shoreline change data must be assembled, analyzed, and interpreted properly for implementation of erosion-based setbacks by FEMA. High-quality data obtained from historical shoreline change analysis should be acquired at close intervals along the coast. Predicted shoreline change from a statistical treatment of the long-term oceanographic information will be less site specific, but interval measurements can be extracted from the data set. In essence, this voluminous information available as output from both methodologies must be entered, manipulated, and output on a personal computer system for ease of operation by FEMA personnel and other users.

Advent of the personal computer with high-capacity hard-disc storage and computerized mapping capabilities makes this technology most attractive to agencies involved in the analysis and retrieval of geographical-based data. These new technologies, which include off-the-shelf Geographic Information Systems (GISs) and user-friendly computerized plotting routines, can be readily utilized by FEMA for their national data base on erosion rates.

A GIS data base management system is based on true geographical locations (latitude and longitude) but also utilizes town/city boundaries, postage zones, and locality names in terms of search and retrieval. This aspect greatly facilitates the utility of such a system, making it readily understandable to the casual user.

Another major advantage of the GIS approach as compared to just "inventory"-type systems is that it can be used to display erosion information in a map format. Computerized mapping virtually has replaced manual cartography at all major companies and government agencies involved in mapping efforts of geographical-based data.

Erosion data in numerical strings (e.g., Metric Mapping; Leatherman, 1983a) or in discrete point format (e.g., state of Florida monument system) can be easily entered and utilized in a GIS computerized format. Therefore, existing high-quality data sets can be entered directly into an already-available data base management system. As computer-based, long-term erosion data for the other coastal states are generated by historical shoreline change analysis, all this information can be incorporated to form a true national data base. Analysis of the historical shoreline data will be useful to FEMA for comparative purposes once the data from the modeling efforts become available. Fortunately, the GIS data management system can accommodate both data sets and, in fact, serve as the host for ancillary information, such as the location of buildings. This system offers the capability for the overlay of erosion data (historical and/or model derived) and insured beach-front buildings on a map at any scale desired. This ability "to view the situation" or gain a quick spatial overview provides FEMA administrators with perhaps as much utility as the actual sophisticated computer-based processing and data base management utilities.

RESEARCH AND DATA NEEDS

The problem of shore erosion is not new, and implementation of the Upton-Jones program can capitalize on a large amount of information from past investigations. Nevertheless, coastal processes are complex, such that the state of the art in predicting coastal erosion remains relatively poor in regard to applying it to the FEMA program.

In order to improve the methodology for assessing beach erosion and the risk of collapse of structures, much more research needs to be undertaken by FEMA and other appropriate agencies, such as NOAA and the COE on the following:

1. determination of the long-term wave climatology through field data collection programs;

2. monitoring of beach response to wave climate variations and episodic events; and

3. more research on predictive mathematical and probabilistic models of probability distribution of shoreline locations by a Monte Carlo simulation of the wave climate, taking into account both the longshore and cross-shore transport.

It is clear that better and longer-term data on shoreline changes should be collected. Specific efforts should be directed toward quantifying storm-generated erosion through prestorm and poststorm surveys as well as the period of beach recovery. The use of remote sensing should be considered for monitoring of beach and dune erosion.

REFERENCES

Dewall, A. E., and J. J. Richter. 1977. Beach and Nearshore Procession Southeastern Florida. Pp. 425-443 in Proceedings, ASCE Specialty Conference on Coastal Sediments '77.

Dolan, R., B. Hayden, and J. Heywood. 1978. Analysis of coastal erosion and storm surge hazards. Coastal Eng. 2:41-53.

Dolan, R., F. Anders, and S. Kimball. 1985. Coastal Erosion and Accretion. National Atlas. Reston, Va.: U.S. Geological Survey (map).

Farrell, S., and S. P. Leatherman. 1989 (in press). Erosion Rate Analysis of the New Jersey Coast. New Jersey Department of Environmental Protection report, Trenton, N.J.

Galgano, F., and S. P. Leatherman. 1989. Coastal Erosion Mapping of the Delaware Atlantic Coast. Delaware Department of Natural Resources report, Dover, Del.

Johnson, J. W. 1961. Historical photographs and the coastal engineer. Shore Beach 29(1):18-24.

Kriebel, D. L., and R. G. Dean. 1985. Numerical simulation of time-dependent beach and dune erosion. Coastal Eng. 9:221-245.

Kuhn, G., and F. P. Shepard. 1980. Coastal Erosion in San Diego County, California. Coastal Zone 80: Proceedings of the Second Symposium on Coastal and Ocean Management, November 17-20, 1980, Hollywood, Florida, ASCE, Vol. III, pp. 1899-1918.

Larson, M., H. Hanson, and N. C. Kraus. 1987. Analytical Solutions of the One-Line Model of Shoreline Change. Technical Report CERC-87-15. U.S. Army Engineer Waterways Experiment Station, Coastal Engineering Research Center.

Le Mehaute, B., and M. Soldate. 1980. A Numerical Modelling for Predicting Shoreline Change. U.S. Army Corps of Engineers, Coastal Engineering Research Center, No. 80-6.

Le Mehaute, B., J. D. Wang, C. C. Lu. 1981. Monte Carlo Simulation of Wave Climatology for Shoreline Processes. Proceedings of Conference on Directional Wave Spectra Applications, Berkeley, California, ASCE.

Le Mehaute, B., S. Wang, and C. C. Lu. 1983. Wave data discretization for shoreline processes. J. Waterways, Port, Coastal Ocean Eng., ASCE 109(2)63-78.

Leatherman, S. P. 1979. Migration of Assateague Island, Maryland by inlet and overwash processes. Geology 7:104-107.

Leatherman, S. P. 1983a. Shoreline mapping: A comparison of techniques. Shore Beach 51:28-33.

Leatherman, S. P. 1983b. Geomorphic effects of projected sea level rise: A case study of Galveston Bay, Texas. Proceedings of Coastal Zone 83, ASCE, pp. 2890-2901.

Leatherman, S. P., and B. Clow. 1983. UND Shoreline Mapping Project. Geoscience and Remote Sensing Society Newsletter. IEEE, Vol. 22, pp. 5-8.

Leatherman, S. P., and R. E. Zaremba. 1986. Dynamics of a northern barrier beach, Nauset Spit, Cape Cod, Massachusetts. Bull. Geological Soc. Am. 97:116-124.

Nordstrom, K. F. 1977. The Coastal Geomorphology of New Jersey. Rutgers University Technical Report, New Brunswick, N.J. 39 pp.

Perlin, M., and R. G. Dean. 1985. 3D models of bathymetric response to structures. J. Waterways Port, Coastal Ocean Eng., ASCE, 111(2):153-170.

Perlin, M., and R. G. Dean. 1986. Prediction of Beach Planforms with Littoral Controls. Proceedings, Sixteenth Conference on Coastal Engineering, ASCE, New York, pp. 1818-1838.

Stafford, A. L. 1971. Shore and Sea Boundaries, Volume 2, U.S. Department of Commerce, Publication 10-1. Washington, D.C.: U.S. Government Printing Office. 749 pp.

Appendixes

A

Upton-Jones Amendment

PUBLIC LAW 100-242—FEB. 5, 1988

SEC. 544. SCHEDULE FOR PAYMENT OF FLOOD INSURANCE FOR STRUC-TURES ON LAND SUBJECT TO IMMINENT COLLAPSE OR SUBSIDENCE.

(a) IN GENERAL.—Section 1306 of the National Flood Insurance Act of 1968 is amended by adding at the end the following new subsection:

"(c)(1) If any structure covered by a contract for flood insurance under this title and located on land that is along the shore of a lake or other body of water is certified by an appropriate State or local land use authority to be subject to imminent collapse or subsidence as a result of erosion or undermining caused by waves or currents of water exceeding anticipated cyclical levels, the Director shall (following final determination by the Director that the claim is in compliance with regulations developed pursuant to paragraph (6)(A)) pay amounts under such flood insurance contract for proper demolition or relocation as follows:

"(A) For proper demolition—

"(i) Following final determination by the Director, 40 percent of the value of the structure; and

"(ii) Following demolition of the structure (including any septic containment system) prior to collapse, the remaining 60 percent of the value of the structure and 10 percent of the value of the structure, or the actual cost of demolition, whichever amount is less.

"(B) For proper relocation (including removal of any septic containment system) if the owner chooses to relocate the structure—

See page 50 for recent change of status of this legislation.

"(i) following final determination by the Director, prior to collapse, up to 40 percent of the value of the structure;
"(ii) the total payment under this subparagraph shall not exceed the actual cost of relocation.

"(2) If any structure subject to a final determination under paragraph (1) collapses or subsides before the owner demolishes or relocates the structure and the Director determines that the owner has failed to take reasonable and prudent action to demolish or relocate the structure, the Director shall not pay more than the amount provided in subparagraph (A)(i) with respect to the structure.

"(3) For purposes of paying flood insurance pursuant to this subsection, the value of a structure shall be whichever of the following is lowest:

"(A) The fair market value of a comparable structure that is not subject to imminent collapse or subsidence.

"(B) The price paid for the structure and any improvement to the structure, as adjusted for inflation in accordance with an index determined by the Director to be appropriate.

"(C) The value of the structure under the flood insurance contract issued pursuant to this title.

"(4)(A) The provisions of this subsection shall apply to contracts for flood insurance under this title that are in effect on, or entered into after, the date of the enactment of the Housing and Community Development Act of 1987.

"(B) The provisions of this subsection shall not apply to any structure not subject to a contract for flood insurance under this title on the date of a certification under paragraph (1).

"(C) The provisions of this subsection shall not apply to any structure unless the structure is covered by a contract for flood insurance under this title—

"(i) on or before June 1, 1988;
"(ii) for a period of 2 years prior to certification under paragraph (1); or
"(iii) for the term of ownership if less than 2 years.

"(D) The provisions of this subsection shall not apply to any structure located in the area west of the groin field on the barrier island from Moriches to Shinnecock Inlet on the southern shore of Long Island of Suffolk County, New York.

"(5) For any parcel of land on which a structure is subject to a final determination under paragraph (1), no subsequent flood insurance coverage under this title or assistance under the Disaster Relief Act of 1974 (except emergency assistance essential to save lives and protect property, public health and safety) shall be available for—

"(A) any structure consisting of one to four dwelling units which is constructed or relocated at a point seaward of the 30-year erosion setback; or

"(B) any other structure which is constructed or relocated at a point seaward of the 60-year erosion setback.

"(6)(A) The Director shall promulgate regulations and guidelines to implement the provisions of this subsection.

"(B) Prior to issuance of regulations regarding the State and local certifications pursuant to paragraph (1), all provisions of this sub-section shall apply to any structure which is determined by the Director—

"(i) to otherwise meet the requirements of this subsection; and

"(ii) to have been condemned by a State or local authority and to be subject to imminent collapse or subsidence as a result of erosion or undermining caused by waves or currents of water exceeding anticipated cyclical levels.

"(7) No payments under this subsection may be made after September 30, 1989, except pursuant to a commitment made on or before such date.".

(b) EFFECTIVE DATE.—The amendment made by this section shall become effective on the date of the enactment of this Act.

B

Glossary

AAER[a] Average annual erosion rate.

ACCRETION[a] May be either natural or artificial. Natural accretion is the buildup of land, solely by the action of the forces of nature, on a beach by deposition of water or airborne material. Artificial accretion is a similar buildup of land by human actions, such as accretion formed by a groin, breakwater, or beach fill deposited by mechanical means.

A-ZONE[b] Flood hazard zone that corresponds to the 100-year floodplain; also known as Special Flood Hazard Area.

BEACH NOURISHMENT[a] The process of replenishing a beach. It may be brought about naturally by longshore transport or artificially by deposition of dredged materials.

BREAKWATER[a] A structure protecting a shore area, harbor, anchorage, or basin from waves.

COASTLINE[a] (1) Technically, the line that forms the boundary between the coast and the shore. (2) Commonly, the line that forms the boundary between the land and the water.

NOTE: [a]Definitions are from the *Shore Protection Manual*, Volume II, 1984. [b]FEMA definitions. [c]NRC committee definition.

CUSP[a]   One of a series of low mounds of beach material separated by crescent-shaped troughs spaced at more or less regular intervals along the beach face.

DOWNDRIFT[a]   The direction of predominant movement of littoral materials.

E-ZONE[c]   An area along the coast where waves and other forces are anticipated to cause significant erosion within the next 60 years and may result in the damage or loss of buildings and infrastructure.

FIRM   Flood insurance rate maps.

GRABEN[a]   A relatively long, narrow area of the earth's crust that has subsided between two bordering faults. In practice it can be one fault.

GROIN[a]   A shore protection structure built (usually perpendicular to the shoreline) to trap littoral drift or retard erosion of the shore.

JETTY[a]   A structure extending into a body of water, designed to prevent shoaling of a channel by littoral materials and to direct and confine the stream or tidal flow. Jetties are built at the mouths of rivers or tidal inlets to help deepen and stabilize a channel.

LITTORAL[a]   Of or pertaining to a shore, especially of the sea.

LITTORAL DRIFT[a]   The sedimentary material moved in the littoral zone under the influence of waves and currents.

LITTORAL TRANSPORT[a]   The movement of littoral drift in the littoral zone by waves and currents. Includes movement parallel and perpendicular to the shore.

MEAN HIGH WATER[a]   The average height of the high waters over a 19-year period.

PERCHED BEACH[a]   A beach or fillet of sand retained above the otherwise normal profile level by a submerged dike.

PLANFORM[a]   The outline or shape of a body of water as determined by the stillwater line.

NOTE: [a]Definitions are from the *Shore Protection Manual*, Volume II, 1984. [b]FEMA definitions. [c]NRC committee definition.

POCKET BEACH[a]   A beach, usually small, in a coastal reentrant or between two littoral barriers.

REVETMENT[a]   A facing of stone, concrete, etc., built to protect a scarp, embankment, or shore structure against erosion by wave action or currents.

SAND WAVE[a]   A large wavelike sediment feature composed of sand in very shallow water. Wave length may reach 100 meters; amplitude is about 0.5 meter.

SCARP[a]   An almost vertical slope along the beach caused by erosion by wave action. It may vary in height from a few centimeters to a meter or so, depending on wave action and the nature and composition of the beach.

SEAWALL[a]   A structure separating land and water areas, primarily designed to prevent erosion and other damage from wave actions.

SHORE[a]   The narrow strip of land in immediate contact with the sea, including the zone between high and low water lines. A shore of unconsolidated material usually is called a beach.

SHORELINE[a]   The intersection of a specified plane of water with the shore or beach. The line delineating the shoreline on natural ocean service nautical charts and surveys approximates the mean high water line.

UPDRIFT[a]   The direction opposite that of the predominant movement of littoral materials.

V-ZONE[b]   Flood hazard zone that corresponds to the 100-year floodplain that is subject to high velocity wave action from coastal storms or seismic sources; also know as Coastal High Hazard Area.

WIND TIDE[a]   The vertical rise in the stillwater level on the leeward side of a body of water caused by wind stresses on the surface of the water.

NOTE: [a]Definitions are from the *Shore Protection Manual*, Volume II, 1984. [b]FEMA definitions. [c]NRC committee definition.

C
Shore Response
Modeling Methods

INTRODUCTION

This appendix reviews the characteristics and capabilities of several shore response models. Development and implementation of the longer-term recommended methodology for predicting shoreline change would be based on improvements to and extensions of these and possibly new models.

The presentation below is organized in terms of "longshore" and "cross-shore" transport models, consistent with the general pattern of individual model development to represent shore response to one or the other of these transport components.

LONGSHORE TRANSPORT MODELS

Longshore transport models include analytical models (applicable to limited situations of interest) and numerical models. Both analytical and numerical models can represent one contour (usually at the mean sea level) or several contours of interest.

Analytical Models

The one-line analytic model was developed by Pelnard-Considere (1956) and applies to a number of cases of interest. The governing equation is the combined result of the linearized sediment transport equation and the continuity equation. Le Mehaute and Soldate (1978) and Larson et al. (1987) have summarized many of the available analytical solutions. Two examples of application of the model to problems of interest are presented below and will serve to illustrate the general capabilities of analytical models.

The interruption of longshore sediment transport by a littoral barrier will cause sediment accumulation on the updrift side and erosion on the downdrift side. According to this model, bypassing does not commence until the shoreline reaches the tip of the structure. Following that time, sediment transport around the structure commences and approaches the ambient value. Figure C-1 compares the analytical model to experimental results obtained from tests in a wave basin. As is evident, good agreement was found.

A second example of interest is the planform evolution following placement of a rectangular beach nourishment project. Figure C-2 presents one example based on the solution of the Pelnard-Considere equation. This solution demonstrates that the longevity of a nourishment project varies directly as the square of the project length and inversely as the 2.5 power of the representative wave height.

Numerical Models

A number of investigators have developed one-line numerical models to represent beach planform evolution as a result of natural effects or human-induced alterations (Le Mehaute and Soldate, 1978 and 1980). These models include the GENESIS model now used by the U.S. Army Corps of Engineers. Because one-line representations have inherent limitations, treatment of cross-shore transport, where necessary, must be by an ad hoc procedure.

CROSS-SHORE TRANSPORT MODELS

A primary motivation for cross-shore transport models (also called onshore-offshore transport models) is associated with the establishment of a zone of impact caused by elevated storm tides and high waves occurring during a severe storm. Some earlier models, based primarily on geometrical considerations, will not be discussed. Various models are reviewed briefly below.

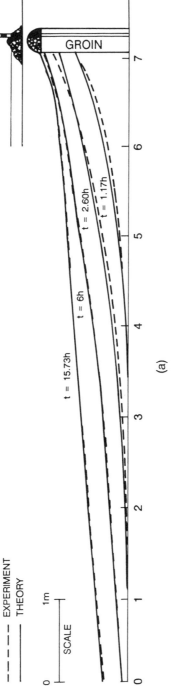

FIGURE C-1 Comparison between experimental and theoretical shoreline evolution. SOURCE: Pelnard-Considere, 1956.

Swart (1976)

This empirical method is based on large-scale wave tank tests. The procedure is complex and involves numerous empirical expressions that, when programmed, make the method relatively straightforward to apply. The only known application of Swart's theory to field conditions is by Swain and Houston (1984a,b) for storm erosion at Santa Barbara, California, and near Oregon Inlet, North Carolina. Their modifications provided for time-varying tide and wave conditions.

Vellinga (1983)

This profile response model was developed to evaluate the integrity of the Dutch dikes against storms and is based on a series of wave tank tests. The required parameters include wave height, storm tide, and grain size. The method predicts the profile for a storm duration of 5 hours; procedures are presented for storms differing from this duration.

Kriebel and Dean (1985)

This model allows time-varying input of storm tide and wave height and solves the equations governing cross-shore sediment transport and continuity using an efficient numerical method. The cross-shore sediment transport equation is based on the profile disequilibrium caused by elevated storm tide and wave height conditions. The model has been evaluated against Hurricane Eloise (1975) for Bay County, Florida. A simplified modification of this method is currently in use by the Florida Department of Natural Resources in its implementation of the Coastal Construction Control Line program.

Balsillie (1986)

This is an empirical method that models relationships for the average and maximum expected erosion caused by a storm based on storm tide rise time raised to the 0.8 power and peak storm tide raised to the 1.6 power. Balsillie's approach provides encouraging correlation with numerous field data.

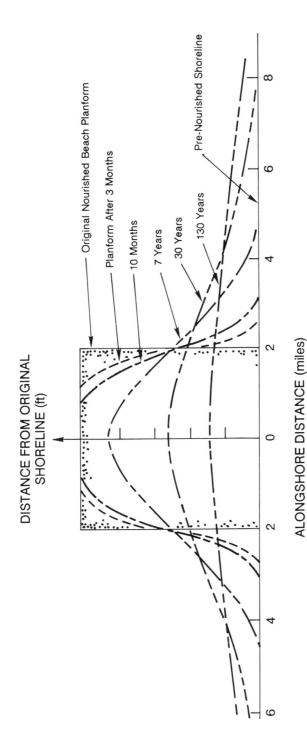

FIGURE C-2 Example of evolution of initially rectangular nourished beach planform. Example for project length, l, of 4 miles and effective wave height, H, of 2 feet and initial nourished beach width of 100 feet. SOURCE: Dean, 1988.

Larson et al. (1988)

This model is based on extensive correlations of wave, sediment, and profile characteristics. The beach/nearshore profile is subdivided into four zones, each with different transport rate properties. The model has been applied to erosion of natural and seawalled profiles. It is capable of predicting single and multiple bar formations. Comparisons/evaluations have been conducted with wave tank data and with field data from Duck, North Carolina. The model also was compared with the Kriebel and Dean (1985) model. Good agreement was found with the laboratory case and the Kriebel/Dean model, but only fair agreement was obtained with the field data.

Federal Emergency Management Agency (FEMA) Method

The method adopted by FEMA (Hallermeier and Rhodes, 1988) for the 100-year storm event references all eroded volumes to the portion of the dune above the 100-year still water flood level (SWFL). The method is illustrated graphically in Figure C-3. The first step evaluates whether at least 50 m³/m of sand per meter of beach length is contained in the dune reservoir above the SWFL and seaward of the dune crest (Figure C-3A). If this reservoir contains at least 50 m³/m, then the dune is considered to not erode through and the geometry of the eroded profile is as follows. The landward portion of the eroded profile is at a 1:1 slope and extends landward from the SWFL to intersection with the dune profile. Seaward from the SWFL, the profile extends seaward at a slope of 1:40. The final seaward segment of the profile is at a slope of 1:12.5 and extends downward to intersection with the prestorm profile. The eroded volume above the SWFL is 50 m³/m, and the 1:40 slope extends seaward the required distance to obtain a balance between eroded and deposited volumes.

We return now to the case presented in Figure C-3C in which the dune reservoir does not contain the 50 m³/m, and it is therefore assumed that the dune will be eroded through. The eroded profile is at a 1:50 slope and extends landward from the dune toe defined as the slope transition between the seaward limit of the dune and the milder beach berm. For this case a portion of the eroded sand is considered to be transported landward; thus, there is no basis (or requirement) for balancing eroded and deposited volumes.

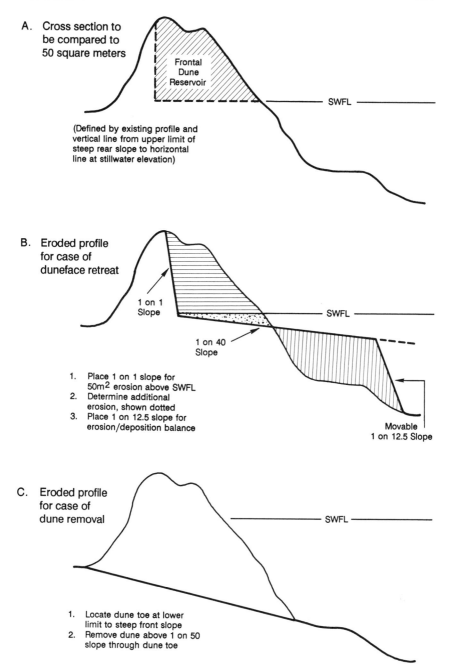

A. Cross section to be compared to 50 square meters

Frontal Dune Reservoir

SWFL

(Defined by existing profile and vertical line from upper limit of steep rear slope to horizontal line at stillwater elevation)

B. Eroded profile for case of duneface retreat

1 on 1 Slope

SWFL

1 on 40 Slope

1. Place 1 on 1 slope for 50m² erosion above SWFL
2. Determine additional erosion, shown dotted
3. Place 1 on 12.5 slope for erosion/deposition balance

Movable 1 on 12.5 Slope

C. Eroded profile for case of dune removal

SWFL

1. Locate dune toe at lower limit to steep front slope
2. Remove dune above 1 on 50 slope through dune toe

FIGURE C-3 Treatment of sand dune erosion in 100-year event for a coastal flood insurance study. SOURCE: Hallermeier and Rhodes, 1988.

Bruun Rule

Bruun (1962) was the first to evaluate quantitatively the role of slowly changing water levels on shore erosion. His formulation is based on the concept of an equilibrium profile, defined as an average profile that maintains its form, apart from small fluctuations, at a particular water level.

The Bruun rule provides a profile of equilibrium with the material removed during shoreline retreat transferred onto the adjacent shoreface, thus maintaining the original nearshore shallow-water profile relative to the increased water level. Hence, the formulation represents an on/offshore sediment balancing between eroded and deposited volumes without consideration of longshore transport.

The Bruun rule can be expressed as

$$\frac{dy}{dt} = \left(\frac{dS}{dt}\right)\left(\frac{w_*}{h_* + B}\right),$$

where y is the shoreline position, $\frac{dS}{dt}$ represents the average rate of sea level rise, $h_* + B$ is the vertical extent of active profile motion, and w_* is the associated width of active motion. Thus, the milder the nearshore slope $[(h_* + B)/w_*]$ of the active profile, the greater the erosion rate. An offshore limit of sediment activity is assumed, thus precluding the possibility of shoreward sediment transport.

Bruun's concept is intuitively appealing but difficult to confirm or quantify without precise bathymetric surveys and documentation of complex nearshore profiles over a long period of time.

A problem with the Bruun rule is that it always predicts shore recession with offshore transport through time as sea levels have gradually risen. However, this is not the case along all shorelines. For example, some barrier islands along the west coast of Florida have obviously accreted over the last few thousand years from the onshore movement of sand (Evans et al., 1985). Sandy material from the shallow shoreface and inner shelf have been moved onshore by waves to form "perched" barrier islands atop of Pleistocene limestone highs. There is no other source of the beach sediment, indicating a reverse product from that predicted by a cursory application of the Bruun rule. The Dutch also have argued that large-scale coastal accretion (thousands of feet of beach and dune) has occurred during the late Holocene (last 6,000 years) during a period of ostensible sea level rise. Finally, there are direct indications of onshore sediment transport by using natural tracers. Williams and Meisburger (1987) reported that glaucionitic sands, which are only available by wave quarrying of offshore sediments, are found on the Rockaway beaches in significant quantities and geographic positions to indicate such a transport process.

REFERENCES

Balsillie, J. H. 1986. Beach and storm erosion due to extreme event impact. Shore Beach 54(4):22-36.

Bruun, P. 1962. Sea level rise as a cause of shore erosion. J. Waterways Harbors Division, ASCE 88:117-130.

Dean, R. G. 1988. Sediment interaction at modified coastal inlets: Processes and policies. In Hydrodynamics and Sediment Dynamics of Tidal Inlets, D. Aubrey, ed. Woods Hole, Mass.: Woods Hole Oceanographic Institution.

Evans, M. W., A. C. Hine, D. F. Belknap, and R. A. Davis, Jr. 1985. Bedrock controls on barrier island development: West-central Florida coast. Marine Geol. 63:263-283.

Hallermeier, R. J., and P. E. Rhodes. 1988. Generic Treatment of Dune Erosion for 100-Year Event. Proceedings, Twenty-First International Conference on Coastal Engineering, ASCE, pp. 1121-1197.

Kriebel, D. L., and R. G. Dean. 1985. Numerical simulation of time-dependent beach and dune erosion. Coastal Eng. 9:221-245.

Larson, M., H. Hanson, and N. C. Kraus. 1987. Analytical Solutions of the One-Line Model of Shoreline Change. Technical Report CERC-87-15, U.S. Army Engineer Waterways Experiment Station, Coastal Engineering Research Center.

Larson, M., N. Kraus, and T. Sunamura. 1988. Beach Profile Change: Morphology, Transport Rate and Numerical Simulation. Proceedings, Twenty-First International Conference on Coastal Engineering, ASCE, pp. 1295-1309.

Le Mehaute, B., and M. Soldate. 1978. Mathematical Modelling of Shoreline Evolution. Proceedings, Sixteenth International Conference on Coastal Engineering, ASCE, pp. 1163-1179.

Le Mehaute, B., and M. Soldate. 1980. A Numerical Modelling for Predicting Shoreline Change. U.S. Army Corps of Engineers, Coastal Engineering Research Center (CERC), No. 80-6.

Pelnard-Considere, J. 1956. Essai de Théorie de l'Evolution des Formes de Rivate en Plages de Sable et de Galets. 4th Journées de l'Hydraulique, Les Energies de la Mar, Question III, Rapport No. 1.

Swain, A., and J. R. Houston. 1984a. Onshore-Offshore Sediment Transport Numerical Model. Proceedings, Nineteenth International Conference on Coastal Engineering, ASCE, pp. 1244-1251.

Swain, A., and J. R. Houston. 1984b. Discussion of the Proceedings Paper 17749 by Richard J. Seymour, The Nearshore Sediment Transport Study. ASCE, Port, Coastal and Ocean Engineering Division.

Swart, D. H. 1976. Predictive Equations Regarding Coastal Transports. Proceedings, Fifteenth International Conference on Coastal Engineering, Honolulu, ASCE, pp. 1113-1132.

Vellinga, P. 1983. Predictive Computational Modelling for Beach and Dune Erosion During Storm Surges. Proceedings of ASCE Specialty Conference Coastal Structures '83, pp. 806-819.

Williams, S. J., and E. P. Meisburger. 1987. Sand sources for the transgressive barrier coast of Long Island, New York—evidence for landward transport of shelf sediments. Pp. 1517-1532 in Proceedings, Coastal Sediment. New York: ASCE.

D
Sections of National Flood Insurance Act of 1968

Section 4001 (Section 1302 of Act)

(c) "The Congress further finds that (1) a program of flood insurance can promote the public interest by providing appropriate protection against the perils of flood losses and encouraging sound land use by minimizing exposure of property to flood losses. . . ."

(e) "It is further the purpose of this chapter to (1) encourage State and local governments to make appropriate land use adjustments to constrict the development of land which is exposed to flood damage and minimize damage caused by flood losses, (2) guide the development of proposed future construction, where practicable, away from locations which are threatened by flood hazards. . . ."

Section 4002

(b) "The purpose of this Act, therefore, is to . . . (3) require State or local communities, as a condition of future Federal financial assistance, to participate in the flood insurance program and to adopt adequate flood plain ordinances with effective enforcement provisions consistent with Federal standards to reduce or avoid future losses."

Section 4012 (Section 1305 of Act)

(c) "[Flood insurance shall only be available in States or areas for which the Director of FEMA has determined that] (2) adequate land use and control measures have been adopted . . . which are consistent with the comprehensive criteria for land management and use developed under Section 4102. . . ."

Section 4102 (Section 1361 of Act)

(c) "[The Director shall develop] comprehensive criteria designed to encourage, where necessary, the adoption of adequate State and local measures which, to the maximum extent feasible, will (1) constrict the development of land which is exposed to flood damage where appropriate, (2) guide the development of proposed construction away from locations which are threatened by flood hazards, (3) assist in reducing damage caused by floods, and (4) otherwise improve the long-range land management and use of flood prone areas. . . ."

Section 4101 (Section 1360 of Act)

(a) "[The Director of FEMA] is authorized to . . . (1) identify and publish information with respect to all flood plain areas, including coastal areas located in the United States, which have special flood hazards . . . and (2) establish flood-risk zones in all such areas, and make estimates with respect to the rates of probable flood-caused loss for the various flood-risk zones for each of these areas. . . ."

Section 4121 (Section 1370 of Act)

(c) "The term 'flood' shall also include the collapse or subsidence of land along the shore of a lake or other body of water as a result of erosion or undermining caused by waves or currents of water exceeding anticipated cyclical levels, and all of the provisions of this title shall apply with respect to such collapse or subsidence in the same manner and to the same extent as with respect to floods . . . including the provisions relating to land management and use. . . ."

Section 4022 (Section 1315 of Act)

". . . no new flood insurance coverage shall be provided under this title in any area (or subdivision thereof) unless an appropriate public body shall have adopted adequate land use and control measures (with effective enforcement provisions) which the [Director of FEMA] finds are consistent with the comprehensive criteria for land management and use under section 1361."

Section 4102 (Section 1361 of Act)

(a) "The [Director of FEMA] is authorized to carry out studies and investigations . . . with respect to the adequacy of State and local measures in flood-prone areas as to the land management and use, flood control, flood zoning and flood damage prevention. . . ."

(b) "Such studies and investigations shall include, but not be limited to, laws, regulations, or ordinances relating to encroachments and obstructions on stream channels and floodways, the orderly development and use of flood plains of rivers or streams, floodway encroachment lines, and flood plain zoning, building codes, building permits, and subdivision or other building restrictions."

E
Minority Opinion of
Robert L. Wiegel

Robert L. Wiegel wishes to go on record that, although he is in agreement with most of the recommendations made in this report and believes there is a great deal of useful information with which coastal erosion zone management plans should be based, he believes that such programs and plans should be a function of state governments, not the federal government, nor should the federal government mandate the inclusion of federal provisions in state programs.

F

Aftermath of Hurricane Hugo

Hurricane Hugo made landfall on September 22, 1989, just north of Charleston, South Carolina. This Class IV hurricane had sustained winds to 135 mph and generated a maximum storm surge of 20 feet. Although storm flooding extended several miles inland, the worst destruction occurred on the low-lying, sandy barrier islands along the coast. These islands were essentially under water during the height of the storm surge (average island elevations are less than 10 feet), and hurricane-forced waves battered the Atlantic Coast beaches. While field survey data are still being analyzed, the first indications are that beach recession averaged over 100 feet, with some profile comparisons indicating 150 feet of beach erosion and complete dune leveling. The damage to beachfront houses was extensive on many of the islands near the storm track (e.g., Pawleys, Sullivans, and Follys islands, S.C.). It should be noted, however, that the true erosional potential of this Class IV hurricane was not experienced because of the rapid forward motion of the storm (24 mph, which is over twice the normal rate of progression).

The importance of acquiring historical shoreline change and

Dr. Stephen P. Leatherman, a member of this committee and the author of this appendix, is also a member of the National Research Council's Hurricane Hugo Post-Storm Assessment Team.

oceanographic data and applying this information to establish coastal erosion zones is well illustrated by the relative damage to beachfront houses in the area affected by the hurricane. The differences in sustained damage at Isle of Palms (north of Charleston, maximum average storm surge of 13 feet) and Folly Beach (south of Charleston and eye of hurricane, maximum average storm surge of 12 feet) was striking. While there was extensive damage at Isle of Palms due to inundation of the island, beachfront houses were generally protected by a wide beach and sand dunes. This storm buffer zone served its purpose well, with damage concentrated to areas where the beaches were narrow and dunes small to absent. The building practices at Isle of Palms were generally consistent with shoreline dynamics, and most damage was inflicted upon pre-FIRM houses sitting on grade. Unreinforced concrete block houses were particularly susceptible to destruction in the V-zone. Often no more than a few blocks of a whole house could be found still attached after the storm. These ill-suited houses appeared to have been "blown-out" by the storm surge and superimposed hurricane-generated waves.

Folly Beach, on the other hand, experienced considerably more and greater damage despite the fact that it was on the weaker (south) side of the storm center. The beach at Folly has been subjected to long-term erosion, so it was already critically narrow before the storm. Residents had resorted to dumping large stones and concrete rubble on their beaches to form riprap revetments, so the shore was heavily armored. These preparations were largely ineffective, as the high surge allowed the storm waves to overtop these coastal engineering structures and inflict heavy damage on the beachfront houses.

The Atlantic House, a local landmark and popular seafood restaurant on Folly Beach, was completely destroyed by Hurricane Hugo. Erosion had gradually whittled away the beach, so an elevated ramp over the water was necessary in order to reach the restaurant. While the hurricane surely swept away the building, it was the long-term erosion that set it up for inevitable destruction. This illustrates the difficulty the general public has in understanding the *process* (the gradual, long-term erosion of beaches) and the total emphasis placed on an *event* (hurricane) in terms of the resulting damage. Certainly better data on long-term shoreline changes, public understanding and acceptance of this information, and the institutionalization of conformance standards for setbacks need to be given considerable attention.

based on emotional reactions and stop-gap solutions often supersede sound judgment. Millions of dollars was spent for emergency procedures to scrape sand off the beach to rebuild flattened dunes without any consideration of sustainability. Perhaps more importantly, state legislators are now calling for rescission of the South Carolina Beachfront Management Act or at least a liberal interpretation of its building setback provisions so that beachfront homes can be rebuilt in their prestorm locations. Certainly this is a difficult time to enforce regulations that are viewed by property owners as "taking." The reality is that their property has been physically eroded away, and any reconstruction must be set back an appropriate distance based on the long-term erosion rate.

National attention is being focused on South Carolina's recovery from this devastating coastal storm and on the application of the Beachfront Management Act. If we learned anything from this storm, it is that the hard decisions must be made before a catastrophe occurs and that the public must be aware of the consequences for poststorm construction. Delineation of an E-zone and implementation of the new FEMA directives in building setback requirements will go a long way to relieve the current dilemma and public misunderstandings.

G
Biographical Sketches of
Committee Members

WILLIAM L. WOOD (*Chairman*) is associate professor of oceanic science and engineering and director of the Hydromechanic Laboratory, School of Civil Engineering, Purdue University, West Lafayette, Indiana. He also serves as director of the Great Lakes Coastal Research Laboratory at Purdue. From 1984 to 1985 Dr. Wood served as chief of the Engineering Development Division, Coastal Engineering Research Center, Waterways Experiment Station, where in 1985 he received the U.S. Army Corps of Engineers's Special Commendation for outstanding service. Dr. Wood received a Ph.D. in geophysics (marine science) from Michigan State University, did graduate work in geophysical fluid dynamics at the University of Chicago, and received a B.S. in applied mathematics and physics from Michigan State University. Dr. Wood's research has focused on coastal hydrodynamics, boundary layer processes, and shallow ocean dynamics. Specific interests have been shallow-water wave transformation, wave instabilities and breaking, vertical and horizontal structure of longshore currents, generation of short-crested waves and their transformation at a coast, sediment entrainment in turbulent boundary layers, stability of coastal profiles in response to storm waves and lake-level variation, and dynamics of submarine canyons. He has just completed an appointment as vice-chairman of the National Research Council's Committee on Coastal Engineering

Measurement Systems and is currently coauthoring a book, *Living with America's Coastlines: Lake Michigan's Coast.*

ROBERT G. DEAN received his B.S. from the University of California, Berkeley, in 1954; his M.S. from the Agricultural and Mechanical College in Texas in 1956; and his D.Sc. in hydrodynamics from Massachusetts Institute of Technology in 1959. His area of expertise is in coastal and ocean engineering. Currently, he is professor of coastal and oceanographic engineering at the University of Florida and director of beach shore for the state of Florida. Previously, he was a professor with the Department of Civil Engineering at the University of Delaware. His research interests include physical oceanography, nonlinear water wave mechanics, interaction of waves with structures, general coastal engineering problems, and potential flow applications. He is a member of the National Academy of Engineering, American Society of Civil Engineers, and American Association for the Advancement of Science.

MARTIN JANNERETH received his M.S. in forest ecology with an emphasis on soil science and ecology from Michigan State University in 1972. He is presently in charge of the Shorelands Management Unit, Michigan Department of Natural Resources, where he implements, administers, and enforces the Shorelands Protection and Management Act. He also consults with local officials, state and federal agencies, and the public on planning assistance, shoreland zoning, and technical assistance on Great Lakes-related issues. He plans regulatory measures, conducts shoreland recession rate studies, delineates high-risk erosion areas, establishes setback requirements, makes official regulatory designations of high-risk erosion areas, and administers appeals of designation.

JUDITH T. KILDOW received her B.A. in political science from Grinnel College in 1964 and a Ph.D. from the Fletcher School of Law and Diplomacy, Tufts University, in 1972. She is an associate professor of ocean policy in the Department of Ocean Engineering at the Massachusetts Institute of Technology, teaching and doing research in technology and policy with special interests in ocean and coastal policy issues. Dr. Kildow has served on several National Research Council boards and committees and was a member of the National Advisory Committee on Oceans and Atmosphere. She is currently a member of the Board of Directors of the Massachusetts Audubon Society, and serves on its executive committee.

STEPHEN P. LEATHERMAN is director of the Laboratory for Coastal Research and professor of geomorphology in the Department of Geography at the University of Maryland, College Park. He received his B.S. in geoscience from North Carolina State University and a Ph.D. in environmental sciences from the University of Virginia. His principal research interests are in quantitative coastal geomorphology, coastal geology and hydraulics, and coastal resources management. He has authored/edited 8 books and published over 100 journal articles and reports on storm-generated beach processes, barrier island dynamics, and sea level rise impacts on coastal areas. Dr. Leatherman was an author of the 1987 National Research Council report on "Responding to Changing Sea Level: Engineering Implications."

BERNARD LE MEHAUTE received his engineering degree from the University of Toulouse, France, followed by an advanced degree from the University of Paris (cum laude) and his doctoral degree with the highest distinction from the University of Grenoble. Currently, he is professor of applied marine physics, Rosenstiel School of Marine and Atmospheric Science at the University of Miami. Previously, he was senior vice-president and corporate chief engineer, cofounder, and director of Tetra Tech. He was appointed by the Secretary of Commerce to the National Sea Grant Advisory Panel for the National Oceanic and Atmospheric Administration under the Ford and Carter administrations. He was nominated by the Secretary of the Army to the Coastal Engineering Research Board from 1982 to 1988, and he was the first recipient of the International Coastal Engineering Award of the American Society of Civil Engineers in 1979. He is a founder of the Coastal Society and is director of the American Shore and Beach Preservation Association. He has published more than 110 papers and is the author of various books, among these *An Introduction to Hydrodynamics and Water Waves*, published by Springer-Verlag and translated into various languages.

DAVID W. OWENS is associate professor of public law and government and assistant director at the Institute of Government, University of North Carolina, Chapel Hill. He works primarily in the land use law area, particularly city planning, zoning, natural area protection, and hazard area development. He served as staff attorney for the Wisconsin State Planning Office. He was an officer of the Coastal States Organization and chaired its ad hoc committee on coastal hazards. He was formerly director of the Division of Coastal Management in the North Carolina Department of Natural Resources and Community Development. He received his M.R.P. in city and regional planning and a J.D. from the University of North Carolina, Chapel Hill, and is a member of the Wisconsin bar.

RUTHERFORD H. PLATT is professor of geography and planning law at the University of Massachusetts at Amherst. He received his Ph.D. in geography from the University of Chicago and also holds a J.D. from the University of Chicago Law School. He served as assistant director and staff attorney for the Open Lands Project, Inc., Chicago, and is a member of the Illinois bar. He has served on other National Research Council committees—the Committee on Flood Insurance Studies, 1979 to 1982, the Committee on Water Resources Research Review in 1980, and the Committee on a Levee Policy for the National Flood Insurance Program in 1982—and chaired the NRC Committee on Options to Preserve the Cape Hatteras Lighthouse.

ROBERT L. WIEGEL is professor emeritus of civil engineering at the University of California, Berkeley, where he was employed from June 1946 until he retired in June 1987. His professional activities concentrate on coastal and ocean engineering, with particular attention on the response of ocean and coastal structures to environmental forces and to the development of environmental design criteria. He was founding president of the International Engineering Committee on Oceanic Resources (advisory to UNESCO) and served for 6 years as a member of the Marine Board, as well as a member and chairman of several Marine Board studies. He was a member of the Coastal Engineering Research Board, U.S. Army Corps of Engineers for 11 years. He is chairman of the American Society of Civil Engineers's Coastal Engineering Research Council and editor of *Shore and Beach*, the journal of the American Shore and Beach Preservation Association. Professor Wiegel (whose degrees in mechanical engineering are from the University of California, Berkeley) is a member of the National Academy of Engineering, a fellow of American Association for the Advancement of Science, and an honorary member of the American Society of Civil Engineers.

Consultant

GERALDINE BACHMAN is familiar with both the coastal management program administered by the National Oceanic and Atmospheric Administration and the Federal Emergency Management Agency program as well as the development process and objectives of builders and owners who develop in coastal areas. She was employed by the federal office of Coastal Zone Management from 1975 to 1977, and from 1982 to 1984 she worked for a private architecture and engineering firm under contract with the Federal Emergency Management Agency to do floodplain and coastal hazard studies. Most recently, she spent 3 years at the Urban Land Institute and was responsible for initiating the policy education program that attempted to bring together conservation and development interests on issues such as ground water, wetlands management, impact fees, hazardous waste, and other such environmental/development concerns. Currently, she is a principal in a small planning/development consulting firm, Marsolan Associates, in Annapolis, Maryland.

Index